think
like a pony
IN THE SADDLE

STEP 2 WORKBOOK

Lynn Henry

www.thinklikeapony.co.uk
THINK LIKE A PONY PUBLISHING

Published in Great Britain in 2011 by
Think Like A Pony Ltd

© Lynn Henry, 2011

All rights reserved. No part of this publication may be reproduced, stored in a retrieval system, or transmitted in any form or by any means, electronic, mechanical, photocopying, recording or otherwise, without the written permission of the publisher.

British Library Catalogue in Publication Data
A catalogue record for this book is available from the British Library.

ISBN 978-0-9566591-1-8

Disclaimer of Liability
The author and publisher shall have neither liability nor responsibility to any person or entity with respect to any loss or damage caused directly or indirectly by the information contained in this book. While the book is as accurate as the author can make it, there may be errors, omissions and inaccuracies.

Think Like A Pony Ltd
Website: www.thinklikeapony.co.uk
www.thinklikeaponyclub.co.uk

Acknowledgements

I would like to thank my family and friends for the important part that they have played in helping me to produce this book.

Thank you to my husband Ged for all of your love and support!!

Thank you to my children for being patient and photogenic.

Thank you to Sarah Gibbon, without whom this book would have never made it past pen and paper.

Thank you again to Su Smith who creates such wonderful illustrations that capture the imagination of everyone.

A special thank you to my girl Friday Sophie Hildreth. Without you, I would not have been able to make my dreams come true. You are my right hand woman!

Thank you to all the children, ponies and horses that have inspired and compelled me to continue the Think Like a Pony Workbook Series. I so hope that you enjoy them and they help you on your journey to understanding ponies.

Written by: Lynn Henry

Illustrated by: Su Smith

Photography by: Lynn Henry

Designed by: Sophie Hildreth

think like a pony
IN THE SADDLE

STEP 2 WORKBOOK

CONTENTS		PAGE
	Introduction	
Chapter 1	Building blocks	8
Chapter 2	Standing still	15
Chapter 3	Walking a circle	28
Chapter 4	Preparing to trot	47
Chapter 5	Hovering trot	58
Chapter 6	Rising trot	73
Chapter 7	Changing direction at trot	88
Chapter 8	Diagonals	99
Chapter 9	Trot on a circle	107
Chapter 10	Hindquarter Yield	116
Chapter 11	Forequarter Yield	125
Chapter 12	Sideways	142

ABOUT THE AUTHOR

Lynn Henry is an instructor of horsemanship, both on the ground and ridden. She lives in West Yorkshire, England, with her husband and four children.

A dedicated senior school teacher, before leaving to bring up her family of three boys and a girl, Lynn has had a lifelong passion for teaching and particularly the teaching of children.

Lynn came to the horse world relatively late in life (35) as a result of helping her children to learn about ponies and riding and was immediately captivated by the relationship between human and pony. She has since dedicated 14 years to horse psychology, with particular emphasis on building a strong foundation on which to develop better understanding, harmony and friendship between pony and student.

Forever in pursuit of a holistic approach to horses, Lynn has added shiatsu and iridology for horses to her list of ever-widening skills.

MY DREAM
A personal message from Lynn

Horsemanship is about more than just riding; it is the ability to understand ponies and horses as well as respecting them and responding to their needs. By being able to communicate with horses, a relationship can be developed. Through this relationship, training is simple and being around horses becomes safe. The information required to achieve this is what I was looking for when I was helping my children to ride and interact with ponies.

Through supporting my children, I embarked on my own horsemanship journey. This journey inspired me to help other parents and guardians to mentor their children so that they could develop the understanding of ponies that my children had.

This book is the last in the **Think Like a Pony Workbook Series** but it is not the end of the support system that **Think Like a Pony** has to offer to children. My dream is that, through these books and the **Think Like a Pony Club**, people will be inspired to achieve their goals with ponies in a way that is fun, safe and most importantly, empathetic. When we look at the world through the eyes of another, we can develop compassion and a real sense of responsibility. This leads to a different way of being with each other, not only with ponies.

Through **The Workbook Series, The Club** and with the help of **Think Like a Pony Instructors**, this ethos can be accessed by anybody, anywhere. This way, we can provide a different approach to horsemanship and we have the opportunity to offer children a different experience. Together, we can build a different future.

Love Lynn

Introduction

When you look at the world through the eyes of a pony, you can understand:
- How they think.
- Why they act the way they do.
- What is important to them.

Time spent with a pony should be safe and fun and this can be achieved if you use a language that you both understand. Through this understanding you can communicate with a pony and form a friendship so they can become a willing and happy partner.

Before you ride your pony try to 'Think Like a Pony'.
What does it feel like to have someone on your back, asking you to go, stop and turn? What does it feel like to wear a saddle or bridle?
By thinking like a pony you can learn to make riding fun for both you and your pony.
If you can learn to understand how to ride in harmony with a pony, riding can become easy, natural, fun and above all safe.
A thinking rider is a safe rider.
A thinking pony is a safe pony.

To parents or guardians:
Children should be supervised at all times. It is important that before a child rides a pony, the pony must be:

1. Accepting of the child and saddle.
2. Controllable and willing to yield to pressure.
3. Confident and able to relax in his environment.

This preparation should take place before you ride. By working with your pony on the ground you can build respect, trust and confidence, so that all the experiences you have together are safe and fun.

The **Think Like a Pony** series helps you to understand the world through a pony's eyes so that you can ride naturally and in harmony with your pony. The workbooks are a step by step plan to help you to build a solid foundation for your horsemanship journal.

For more information please visit the Think Like a Pony website at **www.thinklikeapony.co.uk**

7

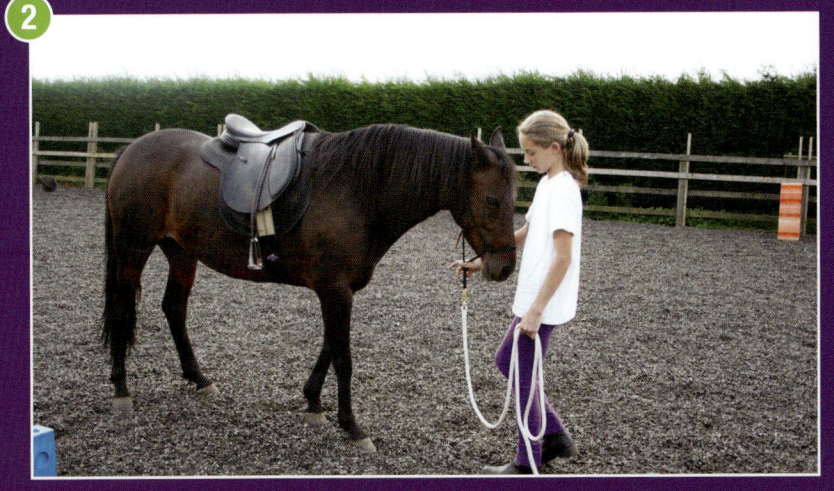

Chapter 1
Building blocks

Working through the Think Like a Pony groundwork books, will have given you an understanding of how to train your pony and prepare him to be a safe, thinking pony.

When your pony understands you and what you expect from him...
when you understand your pony and what he needs...
then you are a team that can achieve anything together!

The **principles** that you used to **train** your pony on the ground are the same **principles** that you use to train your pony in the saddle.

Contact

Terminology or phrases such as "on the bit" or "in a frame" or "in an outline" are confusing and unhelpful for you and your pony. To accept a bit or bridle, your pony must be able to accept and understand contact.

Contact is pressure and relies on you and your pony understanding one important principle.

Pressure asks and release teaches.

I get it! Pressure on my nose means go back!

For example, pressure asks your pony to back up. Release from pressure tells him he has done the correct thing.

When you ride or lead, contact is something that you and your pony share and should allow you to move freely together.

Contact can contain and direct your pony's movement without restricting him. Just like a glass can contain water, but the water can still move within the glass.

You must learn to use contact from your body, then your reins correctly, only using pressure when you are asking your pony to do something!

**The important thing to understand is...
Contact asks and contains, it should not restrain.**

Now you are going to trot and later canter, it is very important that you can use contact correctly. When you ride, the first point of contact between you and your pony is when you sit on him. This is where contact begins with your intention, body language and weight. He will not accept contact or be "on the bit" or "on the bridle" if he cannot first make sense of your body language. This will lead to tension, fear and a loss of balance and rhythm. In short, you will have an unhappy pony.

You should always consider helping your pony to become athletic, making sure that anything you do with him he understands and is for his good. This will help him to become not only athletic but brave, calm and confident. This makes your pony a perfect partner for you to ride and helps you to be a perfect partner for your pony.

Scales of training

Your ground work and early ridden work follows the scales of training which are understood by all good horsemen.

The principles that the scales of training follow are the fundamentals for riding and are the foundation of every relationship with a pony.

The scales of training that most horse trainers follow are:
1. Relaxation
2. Rhythm
3. Supple
4. Contact
5. Straight
6. Impulsion
7. Collection

It is considered by all trainers of all disciplines that the foundation begins with relaxation and works towards collection. Impulsion is often talked about as going forward but if your pony can only go forward, he will find stopping difficult. To be balanced physically, your pony should be able to stop, go backwards and forward. This is impulsion. Collection is when your pony is athletic and can carry himself forward and stop in balance.

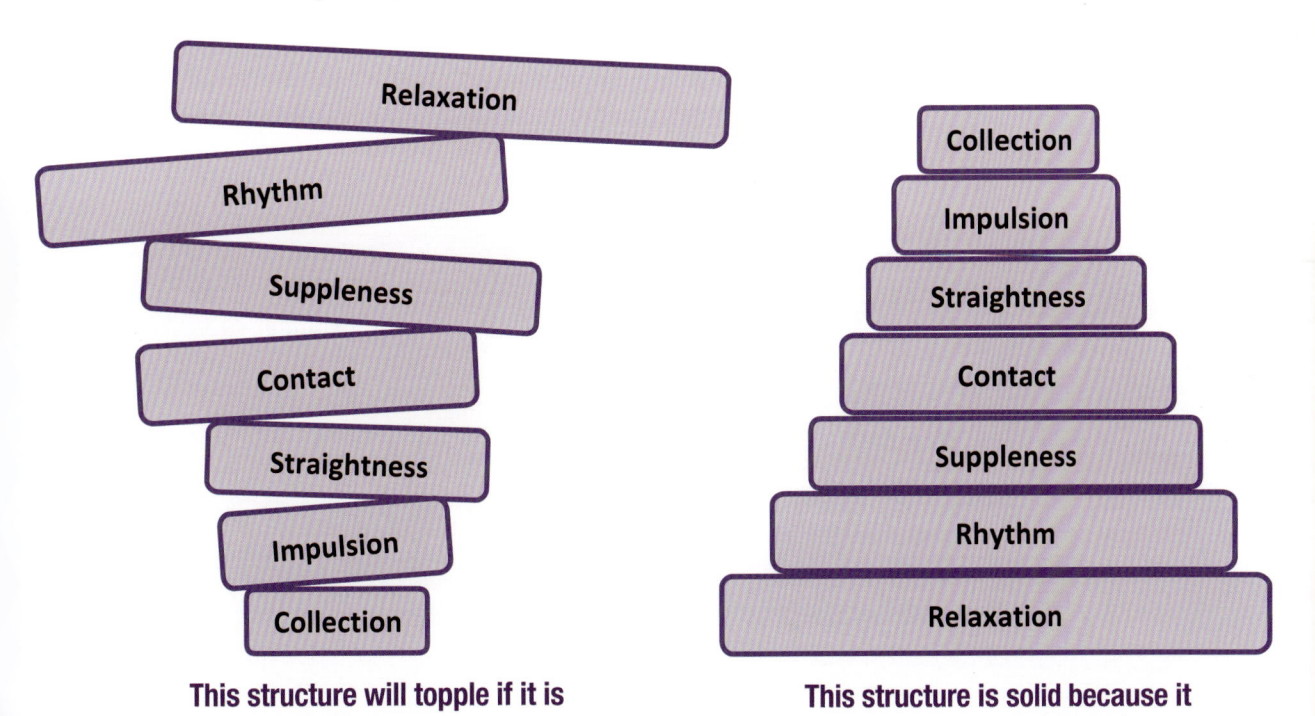

This structure will topple if it is put under pressure.

This structure is solid because it has a strong foundation.

It is important to understand that each principle is part of a training plan and appears in the correct order and in the correct proportion.

If not something will fail in:

- Your relationship.
- Your success.
- Your fun.
- Or even your pony's welfare.

The Think Like a Pony Approach has shown you how to train by understanding and successfully applying these scales of training.

By trusting each other and gaining respect your pony can relax.

When your pony is relaxed you can help him to start to develop rhythm. You can hear, see and feel this rhythm.

When your pony is relaxed and has rhythm, then you can help him to become supple and move freely.

When you learn to share and understand contact you can communicate effectively to further develop his rhythm and suppleness.

When your pony is relaxed, has rhythm, is supple and understands contact then you can help him to develop balance and strength.

Together these things help your pony to become straight. When your pony is straight, you are able to stop, go and turn with ease.

When your pony is straight, he will develop even muscles and can use all four legs equally. The movement of his head, neck and shoulders will be fluid, his hindquarters will be able to push and he will be able to develop impulsion.

When you have all these principles in place, collection becomes possible and feels natural, because it comes from working and riding in harmony together.

When you train a pony you are not only working with his body but his mind and emotions.

Think Like a Pony: how would you feel if someone trained you to jump higher and run faster or dance better, but never asked you how you felt or considered if you were ready and willing for the job in hand?

Think of your training as first connecting with your pony's mind and emotions and then his body.

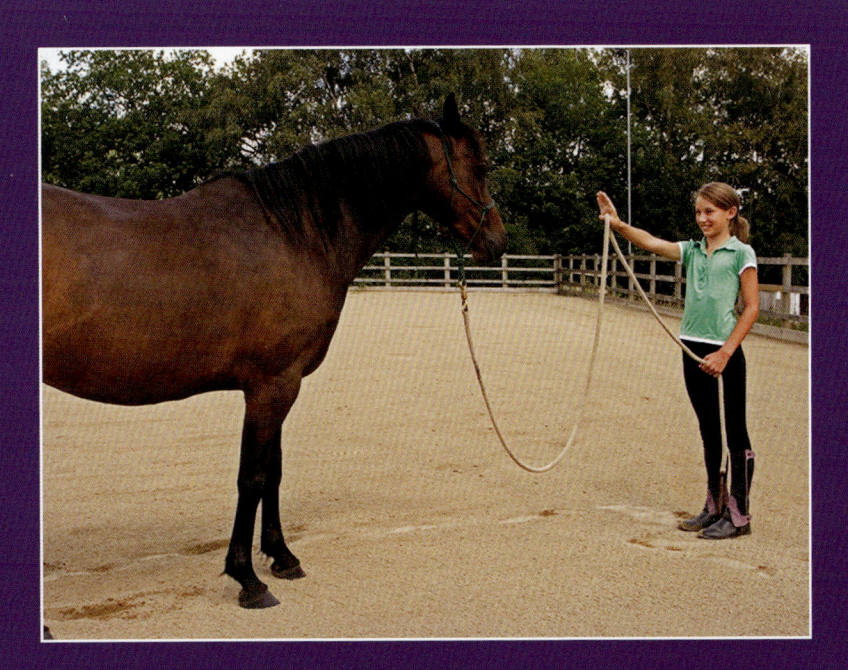

The way to connect with a pony's mind and emotions is through building trust and respect.

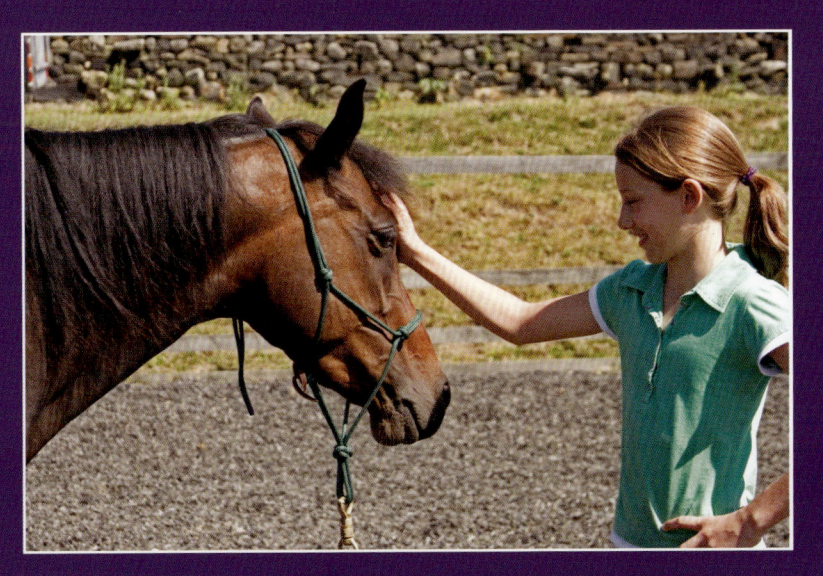

Only when you have this trust and respect can you and your pony relax together.

When training a horse or pony, you should start with the head. The head leads the way, physically, mentally and emotionally. If your pony has a relaxed mind, his head and neck will relax, this is where relaxation of his body begins. Only then can the back relax and the engine in the hindquarters can engage.

By thinking like a pony, your training on the ground and in the saddle becomes considerate, empathetic and above all safe and fun.

Your dream of having the perfect relationship with your pony and achieving your competition goals can come true.

There are no short cuts to building a strong house. You have to start with the foundation and build up. To be the best trainer you can for your pony, you need to be a responsible "builder".

Chapter 2
Standing Still

Being able to successfully manoeuvre your pony and control and direct his movements, both on the ground and in the saddle, shows your pony that you are the leader. This helps to make you safe so that you and your pony can have fun together!

It is also very important to be able to ask your pony to stand still and stay where you want him to be. If he moves when you have not asked him to, he may be trying to be the leader.

If your pony can stand still, then he is more likely to be relaxed.

Your pony may be scared or unsure and find it difficult to stand still

When he does stand still you do not want him to 'nod off'.

This is because he should always be aware of you and his surroundings

If your pony does "nod off", you can tap him or ask him to walk forward.

You are going to use the skills you learned on the ground to practise "parking" your pony and asking him to stand still and relax in neutral. When you can "park" successfully on the ground, you can ask him to stand still and "park" when you ride him.

REMEMBER! The power of neutral! On the ground, when the fiadore knot is in neutral, it means:

"Stand still and only move if the fiadore knot moves".

In the saddle, when you, your reins and your body are in neutral, it means:

"Stand still and only move when I ask you to".

By learning to "park" your pony, you can become more accurate with your signals so that your pony listens to your body language. If you can "park" your pony, then you are helping him to see you as a good leader. Then he can feel safe enough to relax and keep his feet still.

Exercise 1. "Park" your pony on the ground

With adult supervision and in a safe place where you both feel comfortable:

1. With your halter and rope attached and your pony's saddle on, prepare him to ride.

2. Use poles or any safe obstacle to mark an area where you can "park" your pony. Make sure that this area is big enough so that he can stand still in it, but not so big that it is not a challenge.

3. When you are ready, lead your pony from the shoulder making sure that you stay at the drive line. Try not to get in front of your pony's legs or behind them.

If your pony is unsure, allow him to be curious. Let him stop outside of the obstacle to build his confidence.

4. Walk towards the parking spot and stop with him and you inside it.

When you stop, make sure that he does not walk in front of you and that you remain at his shoulder.

Put the fiadore knot in neutral and allow the rope to hang towards the ground. Wait there a few moments and relax together. When you are ready, walk on making sure that you stay at his shoulder.

Make sure that you can do this from both sides.

5. When you can confidently do this, walk towards the "parking" spot again.

Stop in the "parking" spot and make sure the fiadore knot is in neutral.

Now step out of the "parking" spot and face your pony. Make sure that the fiadore knot stays in neutral and the rope is hanging down towards the floor.

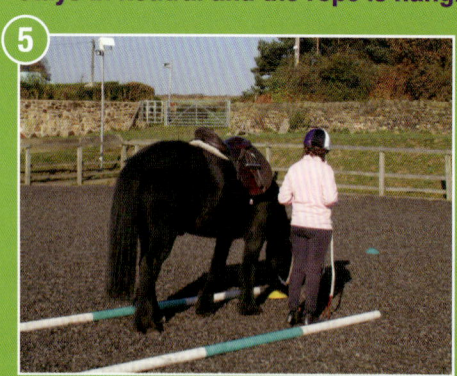

Wait a few moments and relax. If your pony can stand still, allow the belly of the rope to touch the floor.

Have the intention that you want your pony to stand still in the parking spot.

Take a step backwards, make sure your body language is showing him that you want him to stay still.

If your body language is inviting him forward, you will confuse him.

Keep the fiadore knot in neutral, wait a few moments. If he stands still, walk back to him and give him a friendly rub.

This pony is licking and chewing

If your pony moves before you ask him to then signal to him that you want him to stand still. Use a signal that shows him that you want him to stand, for example lift your hand. You can lift and gently vibrate the rope to ask him to move back and stand still.

You can remind yourself of how to use a wiggle to vibrate the rope to back up your pony. Refer back to **Think Like a Pony on the Ground Workbook 2, Chapter 4, exercise 9.**

You will have to slide your hand down the rope to lift it off the floor.

If he first learns to listen to a lift of the rope, you are preparing him to listen to a lift of the reins.

Practise walking further away from your pony. You may be able to get to the end of your rope; make sure that you always keep the fiadore knot in neutral, so that he knows to stand still.

Make it a simple rule to always practise standing still and quietly together for a few moments.

When you can do this, you are ready to ride and park!

Exercise 1a. Park your pony in the saddle

1. When you are ready, mount your pony and go through your check list:

- Relax
- Flex
- Position
- Allow

2. When you are ready, ask your pony to walk forward. Walk past, around and through the parking spot, before you think about stopping.

This way your pony may learn to see the parking challenge as a reward, a nice comfortable place to stop.

3. When you are ready, approach your parking spot. As you approach, think about stopping inside your challenge area and hold that intention.

Use your body language clearly to show your pony what you want to do.

Be determined to resist his movement making sure you allow him to use his back to stop. Feel that you can allow him to step underneath you to stop. Use your breath.

think *like a pony*
IN THE SADDLE

REMEMBER! Breathing out can help you to stop in the saddle!

If necessary use one rein to signal stop and one rein to ask for a little flexion. Make sure you keep the feel of a shared contact in both reins.

Your pony should now be thinking of staying straight as he stops and keeping his nose, head and neck in line with the middle of his chest.

If he stops in the parking spot, release your feel on the reins and try to hold them at the buckle end so that they are loose and your pony can feel they are in neutral.

Rest them on his withers. Make sure you are relaxed and your body is in neutral. This means that you are not asking your pony to go anywhere. Give him a friendly rub!

4. When you are ready, pick up the reins and go through your check list. Prepare to walk out of the "parking" spot. If your pony moves as soon as you pick up the reins, check your body language and intention. It is important that your pony only moves when you ask him to. Make sure your rein position matches your body language.

5. Approach your parking challenge from different directions. Stay parked for different lengths of time. Practise picking up the reins and putting them down. Keep your pony parked.

This way you are checking that you can both relax together. This is like checking the steering, pedals or brakes of your bike before you start to pedal and go somewhere.

If your pony finds stopping in the obstacle difficult, make sure that you spend more time asking him to manoeuvre outside the challenge. For example, by riding around the arena and changing direction as many times as you can.

When you feel he has moved around enough, walk towards the parking spot again with the intention of stopping in it.

If he stops, put the reins on his neck, holding them at the buckle. Relax, breathe and give him a scratch or friendly rub.

> **A good leader has a plan and is determined. Stay focused and you will succeed!**

If he does not stop, try walking fast, then slow, this will help your pony to listen to you. Refer back to **Think Like a Pony in the Saddle Workbook 1, Chapter 12** to remind yourself of this exercise.

Make sure you walk him around and change direction as much as possible when outside the parking spot.

Try to get your pony to want to stop, park and rest.

6. If you are still finding the ridden exercises difficult, work on the ground again or ask your helper to walk with you to encourage him to stop. You can put your halter on underneath your bridle if you want to and your helper can use the rope.

When you can successfully park your pony, make the exercise more challenging as you did on the ground. Make sure that he does not 'nod off' when you are parked. If he does, walk on.

Each time you 'park', make sure you put the reins on his neck so that he learns that this means stand still.

If you are consistent with your signals for go and stop, your pony will learn the correct response and always make the right choices.

When you are confident, practise parking in different places, in between or on different obstacles.

Make sure that you are still sitting in balance so that you are not a heavy burden for your pony to carry.

It is not respectful to treat your pony as an arm chair and slouch on him.

If you want to give your pony a rest, dismount for a few moments and give him a rub.

The exercises in this chapter are explained and supported through worksheets and video lessons, which are available through the **Think Like a Pony Club**.

Have fun!

Chapter 3
Walking a Circle

You know from 'Think Like a Pony on the Ground Workbook 2' that moving correctly on a circle can help to make your pony strong and supple, develop rhythm and balance and become athletic.

Rhythm is very important to the ridden pony.

If your pony loses his rhythm, he will find it difficult to relax.

When he cannot relax, he will become tense and difficult to ride and he may not want to go.

When he loses his rhythm, he will find it difficult to balance himself and he will find stopping difficult. This becomes more important when you start to trot and canter because it is easier for him to become unbalanced as he moves faster.

> **When you ride your pony on a circle you must ride a circle with your intention and body language. When you are truly riding a circle, you can influence your pony's movements and guide him.**

Before you ride on a circle, it will help to learn to walk a circle on the ground yourself to feel what happens if you lose your intention and focus, or your body language is not correct.

Try this! Walking a circle

To the parent or guardian: You can mark out a circle so that it is easier for the child to see where they need to be. This helps them to ride a circle later. The circle should be about 15-20 metres diameter (That's 15-20 large strides across the middle of the circle). The size of your circle depends on the size of your pony and the space you have available. Smaller circles are more difficult.

1. Hold your arms in front of you with a bend in your elbow as if you are holding your reins. Look up and around the circle.

Start to walk around the outside of the circle in a clockwise direction (to the right).

Make sure that you are lifting your rib cage as you walk.

REMEMBER! To breathe, relax your shoulders and imagine your shoulder blades are sliding down your back.

Look up and have the intention that you are going to walk a circle. Turn your eyes, nose, shoulders and belly button on the circle. Look ahead to where you will be in 10 or 12 steps.

Make sure that your shoulders are turning on a circle. Be aware of how this feels as you walk your circle. If you are walking the circle correctly, you will feel as if your right leg comes across your body.

2. **Now put your attention straight ahead of you. Notice what happens to your body:**

Where did your shoulders go?

Did you stay on a circle or did you walk straight?

3. Now put your intention into the middle of the circle.

What happens to your shoulders?

Could you stay on the circle?

4. Now put your intention out of the circle

What happens to your shoulders?
Where do you go now?

5. After you have tried these exercises walking clockwise, then walk anti-clockwise.

Does it feel the same?

Do you have a direction that you favour?

How do you think this will influence your pony when you are riding him?

To walk a circle correctly you must have the intention and focus that you want to walk a circle.

Clockwise

Anti-clockwise

REMEMBER! When you ride your pony, he is a mirror image of you. His nose and shoulders should reflect what your nose and shoulders are doing.

When you ride try to think…
- Is my pony's nose where my nose is?
- Are my pony's shoulders where my shoulders are?
- Are my pony's legs going where my legs are going?

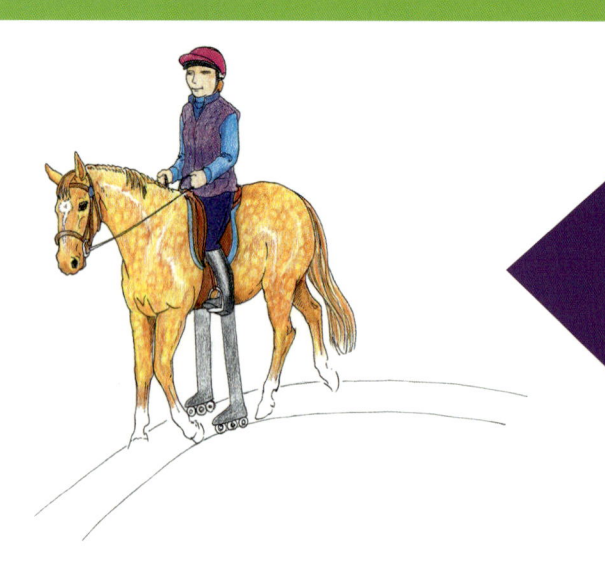

When you ride your pony you have a leg on either side of him. You should feel that if your feet could touch the floor, you would be moving together.

This way if your pony does not stay on a circle when you ask, the first thing you check is yourself!

Ask - "Am I riding a circle?"

If you are using your body language to stay on a circle, then you can use your reins.

Riding circles can be difficult if your pony is stiff or tense. Preparing by working on circles on the ground is very helpful. It teaches you how to walk a circle and helps your pony to use his body correctly.

When you are riding straight lines or circles, you are controlling your pony's body with your body first and then the reins.

When you are riding, it is especially helpful to think:

Head Shoulders Knees And toes

REMEMBER! Keeping your knees in contact with your saddle not only distributes your weight but also helps you to steer with your body. This is because, with your knee resting on the saddle, your bottom can move correctly and influence your pony's movements.

Exercise 2. Riding a circle in walk

With adult supervision and in a safe place where you both feel comfortable:

1. With your halter and rope attached and your pony's saddle on, prepare him to ride.

2. When you are ready, mount your pony and go through your checklist:
   - Relax
   - Flex
   - Position
   - Allow

3. Ask your pony to walk on.

4. Have the intention that you are going to walk a large circle about 15-20 metres diameter anti clockwise.

   Check that you are looking in-between your pony's ears to a point ahead of you where you will be in 10-12 of his steps.

Check your nose and shoulders are turning on the circle. Check that your weight is even in both seat bones and both your feet are feeling for the floor. Both your legs are at the girth, your toes pointing forward in the direction that you are moving.

REMEMBER!
You steer your pony with your body, which includes your toes. Your toes **MUST** be looking onto a circle.

Notice and be aware of how your pony is moving. Follow his walk as you have before, making sure you are light in the saddle.

Ask yourself:

- Is he striding out?
- Is he rushing?
- Is he too slow?
- Is he tracking up?
- Is he making the circle bigger?
- Is he making the circle smaller?
- Is he looking out of the circle?
- Is he looking in on the circle?

Ask your parent or guardian to help you with the answer to these questions.

You may need to try and walk one or two circles before you can answer them.

5. You are now going to use your intention, body language, weight aids and reins to ask your pony to stay on the circle. He may find this difficult, so be patient.

Look where you want to be on the circle and keep your intention to get there. Make sure you turn your eyes, nose, shoulders and belly button together.

You will look as if you are riding your pony between your hands, legs and feet. Your legs should be on the drive line.

If your pony finds this difficult, check where you're looking with your:

- Eyes
- Nose
- Shoulders
- Belly button
- Legs
- Feet

Check that:

- Your weight is even in both seat bones and feet.
- You are light and lifting your rib cage.
- Your rein aids are clear.
- You are not kicking on every stride.
- Your legs are on the drive line. If you kick back you will confuse your pony because he will think that you are asking him to move his hindquarters.

If your pony looks out of the circle, use your left rein to ask him to flex and look on to the circle. Keep a light contact on your right rein.

Make sure you allow him forward and there is no backward feel. Your outside rein prevents him from flexing too far.

The rider is looking on the circle but the pony is not. By lifting her inside rein, she can ask for her pony to look on the circle.

The moment he responds, put your left rein back into neutral near his neck.

Your left rein is on the inside of the circle. When you are riding a circle anti-clockwise, your left rein is known as your inside rein.

When your left rein is on the inside, you are riding on the left rein.

Your right rein is on the outside of the circle and is known as your outside rein.

6. When you ask your pony to flex and look onto the circle, he may try to make the circle smaller. You may feel as if he is falling in on the circle.

If this happens, have the intention and feeling that you can step your weight to the outside of the circle. Your weight will be down into your right leg (on the outside of the circle).

Make sure that you keep looking on to the circle and that your pony keeps looking on to the circle.

Once your pony responds, have the intention to put your weight evenly in both seat bones. Then you are sat in the middle of his back. Be aware of your legs on either side of him "walking" where you want him to go and look onto the circle.

7. If he does not step back out to the circle, check your body language. Are you riding a circle?

Think about stepping to the outside of the circle and use your body language to ask for this. Always use your intention and weight before your leg. This way your pony can try to follow your suggestion before you need to reinforce your signal.

If your pony still does not respond, then use your left leg against his side and use a feel of steady pressure to ask him to step away from your leg. This encourages him to follow your weight signal, which says "follow me back on to the circle".

When you use your legs, be careful not to collapse in the waist and lean. If you do, you will be out of balance in the saddle and will be giving your pony confusing signals.

think
like a pony
IN THE SADDLE

> To stop you from leaning, imagine that you have a glass of water on each shoulder. Think that you must not tip the water out of the glass as you step out onto the circle.

Check your weight is even in both seat bones, you are sat in the middle of his back and riding forward on the circle.

If your pony does not move away from your left leg, increase the feel of steady pressure against his side on the girth (at the drive line) and if he responds, release.

If he still does not respond, check your body language and your feel on the outside rein. Hold him on the circle with this rein.

Make sure that you can ask him to look out of the circle with the outside rein and that you do not pull back with the reins. Lift your inside leg straight out away from his side and give him a little bump on his side.

This is a rhythmical on off, on off with your leg on the girth (at the drive line) to encourage him to listen to your weight and steady pressure. This must be a forward feel and make sure that your leg doesn't bump him behind the drive line. Try to keep your knee on your saddle as you do this. When he responds, sit quietly and walk on the circle.

8. If your pony drifts out of the circle have the intention that you can step your weight to the inside.

Have the feeling that you can reach for the floor with your left foot.

If he responds and follows your weight, reward him and put your weight back into neutral.

Check that you are allowing him forward.

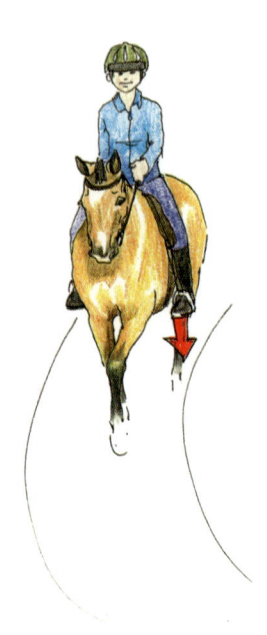

If your pony does not respond and is still drifting out of the circle, then use your outside leg (right leg) against the girth (on the drive line) in rhythm with his walk. Have the intention that you want him to move away from this leg and feel that you can **push**. Make sure that your toes are in the direction of the circle. This stops him from drifting out of the circle.

You may feel as if you are pushing the outside of him around the circle.

If he responds, put your leg back to neutral and continue to ride on the circle

If he does not respond, you may need to use your reins to direct him onto the circle.

As you walk a circle together, you may have to ask him many times to stay on a circle. The most important thing is that you both try to keep your:

- Nose
- Head
- Shoulders
- Knees
- Legs
- Toes

...on the circle

REMEMBER! Your pony is building strength, flexibility, rhythm and balance.

To the parent or guardian:

If your child is young or riding circles for the first time, you can help them by putting them on line. Circles are hard work for your pony and child so make sure you walk with them so that you make the circle large.

You can help by:

- Asking the pony to keep his nose on the circle
- Supporting the child's leg aids to go out onto a circle

Moving on a circle is hard work, so your pony may try to avoid it! Try to make this fun for both of you. Keep smiling.

You are learning to keep your nose, shoulders, belly button and legs on a circle, whilst asking your pony to keep his nose, shoulders and legs on a circle.

9. When you have ridden 2 to 4 circles anti-clockwise to the left, prepare to ride a circle clockwise to the right.

When you are ready:

- **Set your intention.**
- **Check your body language.**
- **Check your weight.**
- **Ask your pony to ride a circle to the right.**

Take the time to be aware of how your pony feels and answer the questions as you did when you walked a circle to the left.

You will now flex your pony to look onto a circle with your right rein. This is now your inside rein.

You will keep him on a circle or prevent him from flexing too far with your left rein, which is now your outside rein.

Walking good circles takes time, so be patient. As your pony becomes more supple and relaxed, he will be able to maintain a circle better.

His nose will look like it is in line with his breast bone

Your nose will look like it is in line with your breast bone

His feet will make two tracks

It will look like your feet could make two tracks if they could touch the floor.

If your pony still finds walking on a circle difficult, look at his body language to help you to find out what the problem may be.

REMEMBER! Your pony is reflecting your intention.

Ride a few circles then walk away and do something different.

If he still finds walking a circle difficult, put his halter on and see if he can do it from the ground and assess:

- **Is he lame?**
- **Is he unbalanced?**
- **Are his feet not balanced properly?**

Take his saddle off and ask him to move on a circle from the ground. This will help you to decide if his saddle could be the problem.

If you are unsure, seek professional advice.

Your reins help you to keep your pony's nose and neck on the circle.

You can imagine that your pony's feet are on a train track. He has to keep all four feet on the track or he has derailed.

Imagine that you and your pony are drawing a circle with your nose, shoulders and belly button but your nose, eyes, shoulders and belly button are always in the middle of the track.

Try making circles fun.

You can practise changing direction.

You can also practise stopping, starting and parking your pony wherever you want.

If your pony is finding circles difficult, then ride half loops.

Part of the loop is like half a circle.

Then ride straight.

Then think of a loop again.

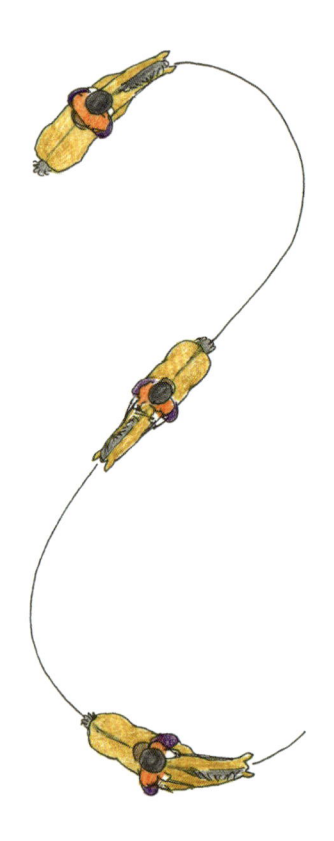

This will also help your pony to become flexible.

The exercises in this chapter are explained and supported through worksheets and video lessons, which are available through the Think Like a Pony Club.

Have fun!

Chapter 4
Preparing to trot

Now that you can safely ask your pony to flex, stop, go, turn and ride a circle, you are ready to trot.

It is important to understand how to move forward with your pony as he trots so that he can move in balance when you ride him. As he moves forward in trot, you have to stay balanced in the saddle and try not to get to far in front or behind the drive line.

If you cannot control your own balance, you will have to use the reins to balance yourself. This will cause you to pull on your pony. He will become uncomfortable and stressed.

If you are out of balance as you trot with him, you may cause him to speed up or slow down.

If you are out of balance, you will sit heavily on his back. This will cause him to feel uncomfortable. He may lift his head and neck to try to get away from you banging on his back, as you land heavily in the saddle.

REMEMBER! When your pony is trotting, he springs from one diagonal pair of feet to the other.

As he does, you will feel this movement. You will rise and fall in the saddle as he changes from one diagonal pair to the next.

> If you do not know how to follow this rhythm correctly, you may feel as if you are being thrown out of the saddle and back down again.

When you are riding at trot, your pony is travelling forward, so you must travel forward with him.

When you sit you must sit lightly and in balance so that he is comfortable and enjoys you riding him.

To see how this feels you are going to practise rising and sitting in a chair. This way you can experience what it feels like to:

- Sit heavily.
- Sit lightly.
- Move straight up and down, out of balance.
- Go forward with your pony.

Try this! Rise and sit

1. Sit towards the edge of a chair, making sure your feet can touch the floor. Balance your weight over you feet and stay upright and relaxed.

2. Look straight ahead and hold your arms and hands as if you were holding the reins. Try to stand straight up without bending or leaning forward, making sure that you do not bend at the waist. Notice how this feels and ask yourself:

   - Did this take a lot of effort?
   - Did you lose your balance?
   - Did you adjust your position?

3. Keep looking straight ahead and holding your imaginary reins. When you are ready, sit down and try to keep looking straight ahead.

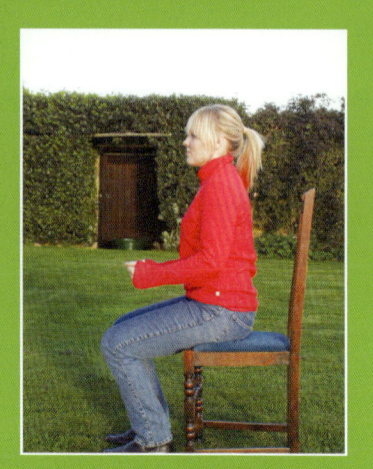

Repeat this a couple of times.

Notice how this feels and ask yourself:

- **Did you sit lightly?**
- **Did you lose your balance?**
- **Is this hard work?**

Get up and down quickly. Does this make you land heavily or become more unbalanced?

If the chair was your pony, you would be rising and sitting heavily on his back. This would be an uncomfortable experience for him.

When you try to stand straight up and sit down, without first thinking about your balance and how you are going to get out of your chair, you need more **muscle power** to move. This can be very tiring.

4. Sit towards the edge of a chair again, making sure your feet can touch the floor. Keep your weight balanced over you feet and stay upright and relaxed. This time have the intention that you want to get up out of the chair. Wait for your body to receive the message from your brain.

Think about dropping your nose a little and softening your neck.

Imagine that your arms and hands are "thinking forward". Wait a moment and feel the sensation in your arms.

It should feel as if they are going to move forward. Remember this feeling.

As you start to get up, rock forward from your hip. Make sure you drop your nose and soften your neck. Lift your rib cage up and imagine your shoulder blades are sliding down your back.

Important: If you bend from the waist you will affect your balance and affect how you are carrying your weight over your feet.

As you tilt forward from your hips, you will reach a point where you can easily and effortlessly stand up. Check that you rock from your hips, not your waist.

Notice how this feels.

In this position you are hovering between rise and sit. If you are balanced, this is not difficult and at any time you could decide to sit or rise.

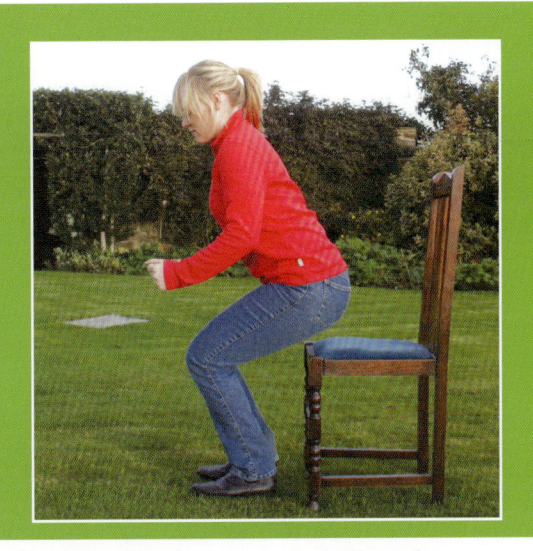

When you are riding, you will practise hovering to improve your balance, strength and flexibility as well as learning how to stay in rhythm with the trot.

5. Now think about sitting down. As you do, wait a moment for your body to prepare itself.

Drop your nose just a little and flex from your hips to sit down. Keep your back soft and as straight as possible and your neck soft.

Notice how this feels and ask yourself:

- Did you sit softly?
- Did you keep your balance?

Repeat the exercise and be aware of your feet. As you rise and sit, your feet remain in contact with the floor. There is no need to push yourself up with your feet. It should feel as if you are pushing into the floor with your feet.

If this was your pony, you would be rising and sitting lightly on his back.

Getting out of the chair is difficult unless you adjust your body and point of balance.

If you move in and out of the chair with thought, allowing your body to flex from the hips, you almost flow or float quietly in and out of the chair.

Easy, effortless and moving together.

To trot in balance you must first sit in balance on your pony's back, carrying your own weight.

Head over shoulders, shoulders over hips, hips over feet.

When you can rise and sit in balance, trotting becomes easy. You and your pony move forward together.

6. Sit back in your chair. Now your legs are not in front of you, stand up.

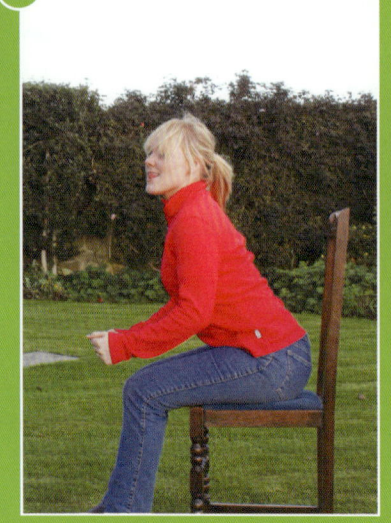

Notice how this feels and ask yourself:

- Was this difficult?
- Did you lurch or throw yourself forward?
- Did you have to use your arms to push yourself up?
- Did you feel as if you would fall back down into the chair?
- Did your head and neck become stiff?

This simulates how out of balance you would be, if you tried to rise out of the saddle when your feet were not underneath you.

7. Now, without moving your feet, try to sit down.

You will not feel confident as you try to sit down, because you are not balanced.

Notice what happens to your feet.

This is a very important thing to remember now that you are going to rise and sit to the trot.

If the chair could throw you up and catch you, then you would not have to be aware and responsible for your own weight and balance.

This simulates how heavily you would sit in the saddle, if your feet were not underneath you.

The chair would do all the work and be responsible for catching you.

REMEMBER! If you sit on your pony as if he is a comfy chair, then you are not being responsible for your own balance.

8. Now experiment with rising and sitting with a backward feeling in your arms and hands, with your elbows "tight" against your sides. This will cause you to arch your back and stick out your chest. Many riders do this and are not aware they are out of balance.

Notice how this affects your balance. Is getting up difficult? Remember this feeling.

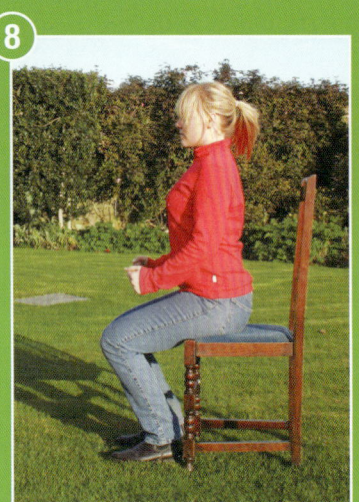

Did you feel as if you were being stopped from going forward?

9. Now experiment with "rising and sitting" when:

- Your head is tilted up and back, repeat a few times.
- Your head is to one side or the other, repeat a few times.
- Your head is tilted back, repeat a few times.
- Your chin is pulled down and in, repeat a few times.

Your head is the heaviest part of your body and affects your balance, especially when you are moving. Holding your head and neck incorrectly will cause pain and discomfort in your body and your pony will feel that you are out of balance.

There is more movement as you trot, so staying in balance takes practise. If you become stiff, you will "bounce off" your pony. It helps to imagine that you have springs in your joints, to help you to move as your pony moves.

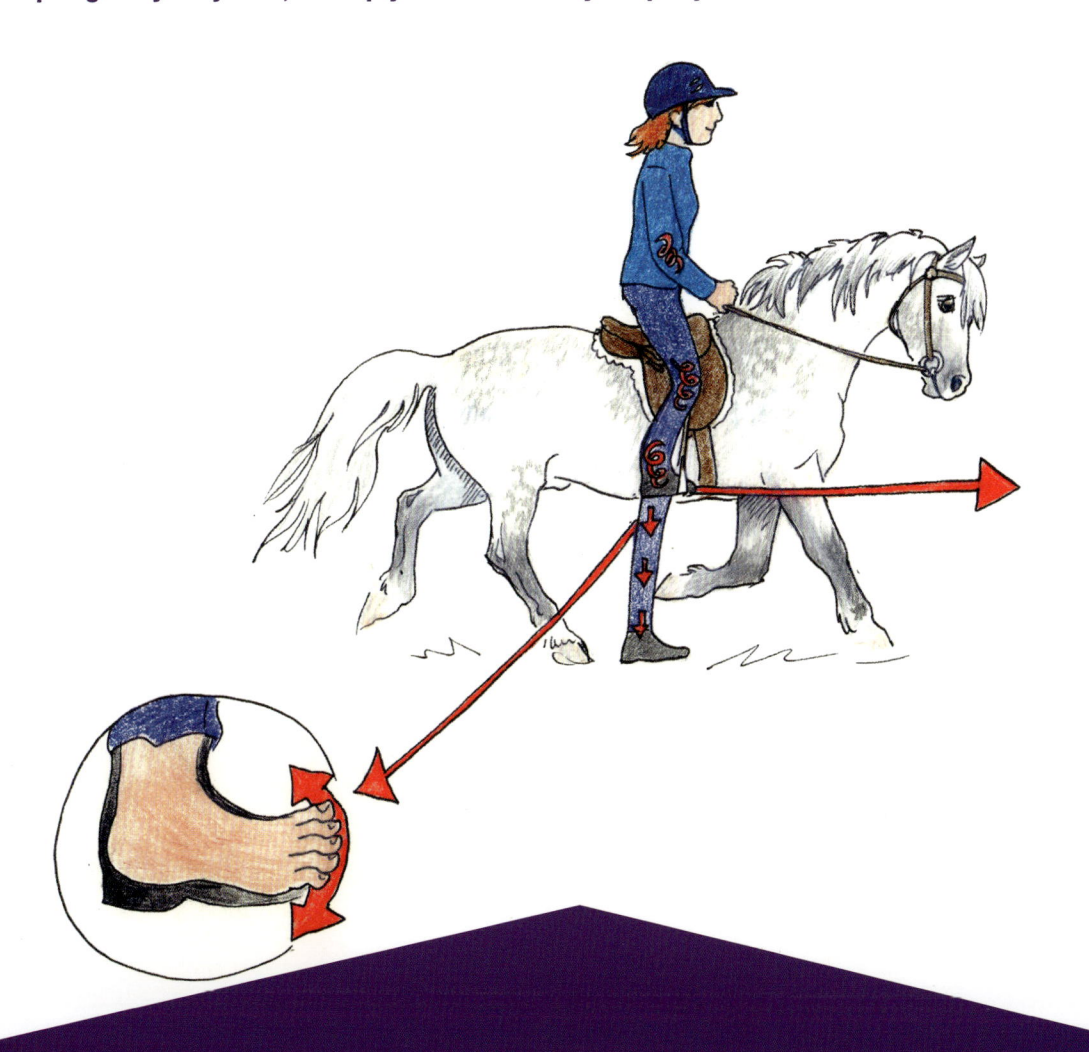

Being aware of how your body is balanced over your feet helps you to balance as your pony trots. To help you hold your balance in the saddle:

- Imagine them facing in the direction of travel.
- Imagine your toes spreading in your boots.
- Imagine your ankles and knee joints are springy and flexible.
- Imagine your feet can grow down to stand on the floor.

Chapter 5
Hovering Trot

Hovering at the trot helps you to work on your own balance and position, and prepares you for rising trot and jumping.

When you are better prepared you become a better partner for your horse and this way you become a better team together. Take your time. Practise this at halt, then at walk, before you trot.

Take time to read all of this chapter before you ride these exercises.

Exercise 3. Learning to hover

With adult supervision in a safe place where you and your pony both feel comfortable, prepare your pony to ride.

If you have never trotted before or you are unconfident, put your bridle over your halter. Attach the rope to the halter and ask your parent or guardian to hold the end of the rope for you. This way you will feel safer as you trot for the first time on your pony.

1. When you are ready mount your pony and go through your checklist.
    - Relax
    - Flex
    - Position
    - Allow

2. To feel the fold at your hip, reach forward and towards your pony's ears.

What happened to your lower leg and foot? It may move backwards!

Feel that you can keep your feet under your seat bones so that you can maintain your balance and stay light in the saddle. Imagine your feet growing towards the ground.

3. When you are ready, put your hands on your pony's wither just in front of the saddle.

Make sure that your knee is in contact with your saddle. Think of resting your knee on the saddle. Check that your toes are pointing forward and your foot is parallel to the floor.

4. Now think of pushing down on your pony's wither and rolling forward onto your thigh. Flex at your hip and raise yourself up, just enough to get your bottom out of the saddle.

Stay there and feel your balance over the balls of your feet.

Try to keep your neck soft by dropping your nose a little. Bend and flex at your knee and hip. Try to keep your back straight.

If you lean too far forward with your shoulders, or your leg is too straight, you will tip and feel out of balance.

Check the length of your stirrup. If they are too long you will find rising difficult. If you want to, you can make them a little shorter to help you with your balance.

Whilst your pony is stood still, practise:

- Rising a little higher.
- Sitting softly.
- Hovering in between rise and sit.

5. When you have felt this balance ask your pony to walk on. Get in rhythm with his walk and take a moment to check how your pony feels.

6. Think about hovering out of your saddle. Holding your reins, as you have done before, put your hands on your pony's neck in front of his saddle.

Push down to support and balance yourself. When you are ready, hover in the saddle and allow your pony to walk on.

Fold at your hips, checking that your back and neck are soft and that you are not folding at the waist.

Ask your parent, guardian or helper to walk with you as you practise hovering so that they can help you control your pony.

Drop your nose and allow your hips and knees and ankles to be springy. Try to stay as close to the saddle as you can.

Think of holding a soft tennis ball between you and the saddle. If you stand up too far out of your saddle, you will lean too far forward and unbalance yourself.

Keep your foot flat in your stirrup with your toes facing forward as if you are walking on the floor. If your leg shoots forwards or backwards, you become heavy or unbalanced. Make sure you push down on your pony's neck. Pulling will cause you to become stiff and you will find it difficult to follow the movement and rhythm when you trot.

If you feel unbalanced, fold at your hips, sit down and try again.

Keep practising until you can confidently hover close to the saddle while your pony walks on.

7. When you are ready, hold the reins in one hand and push down on your pony's neck to balance yourself.

When you can, hold your other hand out to the side.

Hover, then sit and relax.

When you are ready, swap the reins and try this with your other hand.

If you lose control of your foot, sit down and try again.

When you feel balanced, try hovering with both hands out to the side.

Even if you have trotted before and you feel balanced, try this exercise to check if you are as balanced as you think or to improve your balance.

To the parent or guardian:

All of these exercises can be done on line. You can ask the pony to trot by tapping with your hand or using a stick out behind the pony in time with the child's signals. This has the effect of backing up the child's signals by driving the pony forward. You have practised these skills in Think Like a Pony on the Ground Work Book 3.

Keeping your child on line helps them to gain confidence and concentrate on themselves until they can ride off line.

This is **VERY** important so that they can learn to balance independently of the reins.

Exercise 3a. Hovering trot

1. Ask you pony to walk on, and when you are ready (and have practised hovering in walk), have the intention that you want to trot. Imagine that you want to rise up out of the saddle. Sit lightly in the saddle and imagine that you can lift your rib cage up and forward.

   This is your first signal to trot. Give your pony a moment to think.

2. If your pony does not lift into trot from your intention, imagine that one seat bone is rising more and the other one is falling more. This makes your bottom feel more active and takes no more than a thought. If you start to push with your bottom, you will become heavy and your pony will not be able to trot.

   This is your second signal.

> Make sure you lift your rib cage and imagine that your shoulder blades are sliding down your back.

3. If your pony does not respond gently, squeeze your thighs against the saddle

   This is your third signal.

   Give your pony a moment to feel it. If he responds and trots, relax and release your signals, then hover.

4. If your pony does not respond, close your lower legs against his side whilst still keeping your knee and thigh on the saddle.

Make sure this is a **forward feeling** on the girth. Check that you do not tip your toes down and use your heals against his side. This will affect your balance and puts your foot in the wrong place to ask your pony to go forward.

This is your fourth signal.

If he does not respond immediately, use your voice to say "trot-on" or click with your tongue as you did when you asked him to trot from the ground. If he responds and trots, relax and release your signals, then hover.

5. If he still does not trot, put both your reins in one hand and tap him behind the saddle.

Make sure you hold your intention and do not release your signals that are asking him for trot.

The moment he responds and trots, relax, release your signals and hover.

If he finds it difficult to trot, look at his body language to try and understand why:

- Is he in pain? If so check his tack. Check that he is not lame or sore anywhere.

- Is he afraid or unsure. If so check your intention and body language. Check that you are balanced so that he can move freely forward.

6. As you hover, feel the rhythm of his trot. Count "1-2, 1-2, 1-2". By counting the rhythm, you can feel and hear if his trot is too fast or too slow.

If his trot is too fast, you will feel and hear 1,2 1,2 quickly; you will feel as if he is running and not springing from one diagonal to the next.

If his trot is too slow, you will feel and hear 1 a-n-d 2, 1 a-n-d 2. You will feel as if he is not picking up his feet and he may stop at any moment.

If his trot has a good rhythm, it may feel like you can "sing song" Monday – Tuesday – Wednesday and so on.

Allow him to feel his rhythm. If you have trotted on your pony before, you may notice that his trot is now bigger. He may take longer strides.

If your shoulders come too far forward like the girl in the picture, you pony may start to trot too fast.

To slow him down, bring your shoulders back over your feet. Check that your shoulders do not come too far back as this will tilt you and push your legs forward.

If at any time you feel afraid or unbalanced, ask you pony to walk by first slowly lifting your shoulders and then sitting back in the saddle with the intention that you would like to walk. If your pony does not walk, use a rein aid as you have done before. See exercise 3b for more help.

Feel the spring in your knees and ankles as your pony springs from one diagonal to the other.

You will feel and see your knee drop in the saddle first one leg then the other leg in rhythm with his trot.

To help you feel this rhythm, say out loud: Left leg, right leg, left leg, right leg.

This is the rhythm of his trot moving your body. As you allow this movement to travel through your body, you are allowing your pony to move forward in trot.

If you cannot feel an even 1 and 2 rhythm and he is not able to spring from one diagonal to the next, he may be lame. Seek professional help if you are unsure.

If you find hovering in trot difficult, you can shorten your stirrups one or two holes.

This helps your joints to be more springy and will help you to balance and feel your pony's movement.

If your pony stops when you did not ask him to, ask him to trot again.

When you are hovering, you do not have to trot for long. Short balanced trots are better than trotting for a long time out of balance. Transitions from walk to trot then back to walk will help you and your pony to improve your balance. Ask your helper to check your balance and give you feedback.

7. **When you are confident and balanced, you can stop pushing down on his neck.**

Keep your knee on the saddle; this helps to prepare you to rise.

First stop pushing down on your pony's neck with one hand.

With your free hand hold your rein just above your pony's neck and out in front of you. Swap hands. Is one hand easier than the other?

8. When you feel confident, hold both hands out in front of you.

Make sure your hands:
- Stay a pair.
- Stay the same height above the saddle.
- Stay the same width apart, about as wide as your pony's neck.
- Keep a light contact with a forward feel on the rein.

Make sure that you:
- Stay hovering and balanced.
- Keep your back, neck, shoulders and elbows relaxed and soft.
- Keep your toes pointing forward and your feet flat on the floor.

Notice how this feels:

Do your hands move?

Do both hands feel the same?

If you feel unbalanced or your pony trots too fast, bring your shoulders up to slow down.

If you need to at any time, balance yourself by pushing on your pony's neck.

As you hover and follow your pony's trot forward with your body and your hands, your contact is shared and steady. Your hands will look as if they are staying still as you move forward together.

If you try to use the reins before you are balanced, you will use the reins to balance yourself!

Exercise 3b. Preparing to Walk

1. To come back to walk, first have the intention that you want to walk and feel your body prepare. When you are ready, sit down and think about stopping. Breathe out loudly. This helps you to relax.

   Slowly sit back in the saddle and then **slowly** lift your shoulders so that you are sat upright. Even if your pony is determined to trot, resist his movement with your intention and body to show him that you want to walk. Think about stopping your bottom from following your pony's trot movement. This affects your weight distribution and is a signal for your pony to stop moving forward in trot.

> Imagine that you are dropping an anchor from your foot to the floor. Think of keeping your bottom still.
> **This is your first signal.**
> Give him a moment to think.

The moment he walks, relax and tell him he is a good pony. Walk on then stop when you are ready.

Make sure that you keep your hands near his neck in front of the saddle. Keep your elbow soft and supple, this way you can keep the reins still.

If your hands move up or down, backwards or forwards in and out, then you are finding it hard to balance or you are tense.

If your elbows go behind your body, then you will have a lot of backward movement on the reins. This means that you will be pulling!

Think that your arms are travelling down towards your pony's mouth. It will also help to imagine that the reins are extension of your arms and that they can follow or push your pony forwards as he trots. You must be relaxed and soft in your wrists, elbows and shoulders.

Think of a flexible soft spring. Imagine your joints are soft and springy.

If you are stiff, you will not be able to move with your pony and stay in balance.

You will have to lift your hands as you trot.

You know you are becoming balanced when:

- You can maintain a light contact.
- You have a forward feel on the rein.
- Your hands are not lifting up and down.
- Your hands are equal, you are becoming balanced.

2. If your pony does not respond to your body language, keep the contact on one rein. Have the feeling that this rein is asking "stop trotting". You should have a feel of "holding" him and not "pulling" him.

This is your second signal.
Give him time to think.

The moment he responds to this feel and walks, relax. Tell him he is a good pony and walk on.

3. If he still does not respond, keep resisting his trot with your body and hold with one rein. Now bring your other rein out towards his hindquarters. Make sure you **lift** the rein and direct it out towards his hip.

You practised this emergency flex rein in **Think Like a Pony in the Saddle Workbook 1, Chapter 10.**

When you have stopped take a few moments to rebalance yourself.

Making a transition from hover trot to walk should be as simple as bringing your shoulders up and sitting back in the saddle!

If your pony is finding the transition from trot to walk difficult, check that you are not tense and causing him to worry! Check that you are not kicking or squeezing him, making sure that you try to breathe out loudly through your transition. Like a sigh!

If you are consistent and take your time, your pony will respond to your body language and stop trotting as you stop trotting.

If he puts his head up as he comes down to walk, make sure that:

- You are not banging down on his back.
- His saddle is not too tight or pinching him.
- Your contact on the rein is allowing him forward.

It is important to practise asking your pony to:

- Trot
- Hover
- Walk
- Stop

Do this as much as possible to improve your balance, flexibility and strength.

Make sure you ask your helper to watch you and give you feedback so that you know how you are doing. Ask them to check that your legs are not slipping back and your toes are not turning out or pointing down.

You are trying to get your pony to respond to your light signals.

You do not want to keep using rhythm signals to remind him to trot! Or keep flexing him to stop trotting.

If you are consistent in the way that you ask for your transitions, up to trot or down to walk, your pony will soon learn to listen for the lightest cue.

The exercises in this chapter are explained and supported through worksheets and video lessons, which are available through the **Think Like a Pony Club.**

Well done!

Chapter 6
Rising trot

Hovering in the saddle whilst your pony trots has allowed you to experience how it feels to follow the movement and spring of his trot rhythm.

You are now going to rise and sit in trot, in the saddle in time with your pony's rhythm.

This is called rising trot.

It is important to understand how to move forward with your pony so that he can move freely forward and in balance when you ride him.

You will rise and sit in time with his spring from one diagonal pair to the next diagonal pair.

When you rise and sit in the saddle as your pony trots forward, it is important that you move forward with him.

Remember when you simulated rising and sitting in a chair, you were preparing yourself for rising trot.

When you are first learning to rise to the trot in balance, you may bring your shoulders a little more forward than you need to and that's OK.

Rising forward is better than rising straight up and down. Trying to look perfectly upright makes you out of balance and heavy. This makes carrying you in trot an uncomfortable experience for your pony.

Remember how heavy you were when you practised this on a chair.

Read through the next chapter carefully before you ride. As you are reading, imagine rising and sitting to the trot.

Exercise 4. Rising and sitting to the trot

With adult supervision and in a safe place where you both feel comfortable:

1. Prepare your pony to ride.

2. When you are ready, mount your pony and go through your checklist.

- **Relax**
- **Flex**
- **Position**
- **Allow**

To think about rising it will help you to think of taking your belly button up and forward over your pony's neck as you rise.

3. When you are ready, ask your pony to walk on.

As you walk, feel your thigh move against the saddle and your knees drop with each stride, left and then right.

Your thigh should lie softly against your saddle.

You are going to imagine that as you rise out of the saddle, you can roll forward onto your thigh.

This way your weight is carried forward on your knee and thigh and this contact helps you to balance yourself as you rise.

If your knee comes off the saddle, you will not be able to balance as you rise and your feet and lower legs will swing backwards and forwards. You may even lose control of your foot and your toes may point down and / or out. You will be heavy and your pony will be uncomfortable.

4. When you are ready, go through your phases to ask your pony to trot. When your pony trots, you will feel him lift you out of the saddle.

When you feel this lift, it is your cue to rise. Flex at your hip, drop your nose, roll on your thigh and rise forwards and up. As your pony trots, you will feel as if he is lifting you out of the saddle.

Feel the spring and rise in your saddle.

You do not have to rise far out of the saddle. If you do, you will unbalance yourself and your pony.

If your body is balanced over your feet, your thigh and knee is on the saddle, you will not need to use your reins to balance yourself. If you lose your balance, push down on your pony's neck to rebalance yourself.

As you rise and sit, your hands and arms should be thinking forward to follow your pony's movement and to allow him to trot freely. Imagine that your reins are sticks and are an extension of your arms and hands. This will help you to imagine a "pushing feeling" forward.

If your hands and arms lift up and down, your pony will feel this and be confused. Your pony is not moving up and down, he is moving forward!

You should be able to rise up in your saddle and allow your knees, hips and ankles to flex, your shoulders slightly forward.

Think of your knees, hips and ankles moving like a spring.

Remember the idea of holding a duckling in your hands, when you hold your reins. This way you can maintain and share a steady contact between you and your pony as you rise.

Rising is like "getting out of a chair with as little effort as possible". Balance on your knee and you will rise with ease.

When you can rise, you do not need to push yourself up from your feet.

If you are pushing yourself up from your feet, you are trying too hard.

5. To sit lightly, drop your nose a little to soften your neck. Flex at your hip and knee and put your bottom into the saddle.

Keep your hands "thinking forward" and keep them in front of the saddle.

If you are in balance, you will sit softly.

When you are practising this rise and fall, you can think of:

- Keeping space under your chin, as if you had space for a soft tennis ball there.
- Lifting up and forward from the top of your hat, as if you could grow up to the sky.
- Keeping space behind your knee joint so it stays open as you trot.
- Keeping your body balanced.
- Moving forward with your pony.

Make sure you keep looking forward and keep your neck soft.

think *like a pony*
IN THE SADDLE

> **6.** Try to feel the rhythm of the trot and sit softly in rhythm with your pony as he springs from one diagonal pair of feet to the other.

To help you to keep a steady, forward feeling contact with your pony, think of the energy in your arm going forward towards your pony's mouth.

This way you will learn to contain, not restrain or stop your pony's movement.

This is the same if your pony is wearing a bitted or bitless bridle.

Keep your chest open and your shoulders soft. Feel your shoulder blades moving down your back and keep your neck soft.

Ask your helper how you are doing.

Can you:

- Feel your knees flex as your pony trots?
- Be aware of your feet in your stirrups?
- Feel your feet facing in the same direction as your pony's feet?
- Imagine that your toes can spread in your boots like a frog's feet?
- Be aware of your point of balance?
- Feel your thigh roll on your saddle as you rise?
- Feel the energy from your hip to your toes come down your leg?
- Feel your foot in the stirrup and imagine that it could grow down to the ground, landing flat and balanced?
- imagine that your reins are two sticks pushing your pony forward.

If you push your heels down or your toes up, your legs become tense. This will cause your thigh to come too far forward and you will be out of balance as you rise and sit. You will be heavy in the saddle and get behind the drive line.

If your toes are down and your heels are up, you will tip forward and will be out of balance when you rise and sit in the saddle.

This will put you in front of the drive line. Your pony will feel heavy and may even slow down.

REMEMBER! When your feet are out of balance, you cannot balance your body over them.

If at any time you feel unbalanced or lose the rhythm of the trot, hover. Feel the rhythm and then try to rise and sit again.

This rider is hovering.

7. Make sure you look ahead over the tips of your pony's ears, with your nose tipped down a little to soften your neck and back. This way you will keep your back soft and springy.

As you are learning to rise and sit, you may look as though you are rising a little too far forward and your back may look round; this does not matter. You are learning to move with your pony so that he can move with you.

While you are riding your pony like this, he may feel the need to stretch. If he does, offer your hands forward, so he can stretch his neck and back.

When he has finished stretching, put your hands and arms back again.

You may see him using his tummy muscles to lift his back. The line of muscle you can see in this picture behind the rider's ankle is called the heave line. If you can see these muscles, it is a good sign that your pony is using his tummy muscles to lift his back.

8. When you are ready, prepare yourself to ask your pony to walk. First think about trotting slower. Lift your shoulders and sit back into the saddle.

Imagine walking and resisting his rhythm of trot.

REMEMBER! If you try to stop too fast, you will lose your balance and rely on the reins to stop.

Have the feeling that your legs can grow down to the ground and resist his movement.

Growing up will make you feel light, so your pony can use his back to stop.

Growing down helps you to feel anchored and stable, so that you can resist his movement.

Make sure that you are not slumping or collapsing in the saddle.

Think of sitting tall and not leaning forward.

This way, your shoulders will help you to resist your pony's forward movement whilst you stay in balance.

> Imagine that you would like to walk forward with your pony.
>
> Imagine your feet growing towards the floor, as your upper body lifts upwards. Give your pony time to feel this.

If he walks, that is fantastic! Give him a rub on his withers, relax and walk with him.

If he does not walk you should go through your "stop phases" as you have done before. If he does not stop from your body language, then REMEMBER:

- One rein asks for stop.
- One rein asks for flexion.

Be prepared to ask him to flex his head all the way to his hips and move on a small circle if he does not respond.

To the parent or guardian:

If your child is on line, you can help the pony to make a transition from trot to walk by giving him a backward feel on the rope. If necessary you can make the circle smaller.

9. When you come down to walk, allow him to walk forward for a few strides and then ask him to stop.

Give him a rub. You have done really well.

When you practise, think of how you can help your pony to trot freely by staying in balance and rhythm with him. Shout, sing or say the rhythm of trot in your head.

If your pony trots too fast:

Rise and sit slower and do not rise as high. Try to get him to listen to the rhythm of your body rising and sitting. If he does not listen to you, give him a feel on one rein to say slow down. This is like a squeeze to give a feeling of "hold". When he slows, make sure that you release your feel on the rein which is asking him to slow down.

If your pony trots too slow:

Check that your contact on the reins is allowing him forward. Have the feeling you can put more energy into your body. Imagine that you want to 'spring' forward and cover the ground together. Smiling helps you to relax, so make sure that you smile.

If he does not respond to your body, then as you sit, squeeze with your lower leg against his side. Make sure your leg has a forward feel on the girth. As soon as he responds, release the feel of your leg.

This way he knows he has done the correct thing.

If he does not listen to your leg, tap him with your hand or stick behind the saddle. The worst thing you can do when you are trotting is to "kick or squeeze on every stride". If you ask him forward on every stride, you may push him out of his natural rhythm.

REMEMBER! **To always ask with a light signal or aid. Be consistent and prepared to use a stronger signal whenever he does not listen. Reward him when he does the correct thing by releasing your signals.**

How would you feel if someone urged you on with every stride that you took?

If you do not release your signals when your pony does the right thing, your pony will become "dull to the leg."

He will never know if he has done the correct thing because you will always be asking with your leg.

When your leg slips back, you are out of balance and making it more difficult for him to move forward. Check that your leg is asking your pony forward.

If your leg slips back or you tip your toe down and use your heel, you will be "talking" to your pony's hindquarters. This will confuse him.

When you practise staying in balance your pony will improve his trot.

REMEMBER! You and your pony are a mirror image of each other.

Hovering helps your pony to relax his muscles, so it is good to include this as part of your warm up before you start rising and sitting to the trot.

When you make transitions from trot to walk to stop, think about getting in time with your pony's transitions. If you lose balance, hover through transitions to stop yourself banging on your pony's back. When your balance improves, you can go back to sitting through your transitions. Sit down gently when you stop and give your pony a rub.

At first it does not matter where you go as long as you are safe and can stop whenever you want. Even if you have done rising trot before, these exercises will help you become more balanced and help your pony to move more freely.

By improving your balance in trot, your pony will cover more ground and find it easier to flex his joints and swing his back. You will not have to "kick him" or "squeeze him" as you sit because you will be moving freely together.

This way your pony will start to feel that you are moving together and you will begin to influence where he is going.

The exercises in this chapter are explained and supported through worksheets and video lessons, which are available through the **Think Like a Pony Club.**

Well done!

Chapter 7
Changing direction at trot

You have influenced your pony to change direction by using:

- Your intention, then...
- Your body language, then...
- Your rein aid.

Now your pony is trotting and moving a little faster, you must be balanced and moving with him before you try to influence where he is going.

If you are in balance with your pony, he will be more willing to turn.

Now that you are trotting, it is even more important to use your intention and body language clearly so that you can influence your pony's direction effortlessly. Always try to think:

- My pony's nose goes where my nose goes.
- My pony's shoulders go where my shoulders go.
- My pony's feet go where my feet go.

Exercise 5. Changing direction at trot

With adult supervision and in a safe place where you both feel comfortable:

1. With your halter and rope attached and your pony's saddle on, prepare him to ride

2. When you are ready mount your pony and go through your checklist.

    • Relax
    • Flex
    • Position
    • Allow

3. When you are ready, ask your pony to walk on. Make sure that you relax, breathe and smile. Get in rhythm with his walk then practise getting in time with his front legs to change direction left and right. If you need to remind yourself of this exercise, refer to Think Like a Pony in the Saddle Workbook 1, Chapter 14.

4. When you are ready, prepare yourself for trot and go through your phases to ask your pony to trot. Look through the tip of his ears to where you are going together. Feel your nose is his nose, your shoulders are his shoulders and your feet are his feet. Keep your hands a pair.

This weight shift is your pony's first signal to change direction.

think *like a pony*
IN THE SADDLE

5. Feel his rhythm and check it is not too slow or too fast.

   When you can feel an even rhythm, you are ready to change direction.

6. Have the intention that you want to change direction.

   Look into the direction that you want to go, making sure you turn your body naturally and smoothly. Look and turn your eyes, nose, shoulders and belly button together. Feel that you are stepping in time with him as you turn.

   Step out in time with your pony to turn.

Think of: **Head Shoulders Knees And toes**

This allows your weight to shift in the saddle.

90

This weight shift and change in your body language is your pony's first signal to change direction.

If he responds and changes direction, that is excellent. Tell him he is a good pony and look straight ahead again, your shoulders and his shoulders should be travelling straight.

Keep trotting.

7. If he does not respond, feel that you can use your outside leg to try to turn him, using a feel of steady pressure. Feel as if you can turn your toes in the direction you want to go. Think "push" to help your pony to turn.

This is your second signal.

If you are turning to the left, then think that you can push your pony around with your right leg. This must be a forward feeling on his girth. To help you get this feel, you can step forward with your right foot in time with your pony's leg. Feel as if the toes of your left foot can point to the right. It is easier to feel and influence your pony as you sit.

Use your left leg and foot to push your pony to the right.

8. Wait a moment to see if he responds and if he does not, get ready to use your rein.

REMEMBER! If you are changing direction to the right, then use your right rein.
REMEMBER! If you are changing direction to the left, then use your left rein.

Lift your rein just enough so your pony can feel that you want him to look in a new direction.

This is your third signal. Makes sure that you maintain your body language and you are looking up and into the direction that you want to go.

If he responds and changes direction, well done.

Tell him he is a good pony, look straight ahead, making sure his shoulders mirror your shoulders. Put your rein back into neutral and trot on.

9. If he does not change direction, lift your rein a little higher and away from his neck. This will give him a stronger feel to flex just a little and look into a new direction. **This is your fourth signal.**

When he responds and changes direction, tell him he is a good pony, look straight ahead, making sure his shoulders mirror your shoulders. Put your rein back into neutral and trot on.

Change direction to the left and to the right. Make sure that you start with the intention to change direction.

REMEMBER! Think "step-push" to change direction in time with your pony. This way your pony will start to respond to your light aids.

If you are finding changing direction difficult, make sure that:

- You have turned your shoulders. Lift up your rib cage making sure you turn from your hips.
- You are not pulling your pony with the rein to change direction.
- You are looking up into the direction you want to go.
- You lift your rein with an intention to direct your pony.
- You go back into neutral each time you change direction; go straight for a few strides before you change direction again. This way your pony has time to adjust his balance and prepare himself to move in a new direction.

If you look down or use your rein with a downwards feel, you will affect your weight in the saddle. Your pony will feel this and be confused.

REMEMBER! If you collapse in your rib cage, you will turn from your waist; you will be heavy in the saddle and your pony will be confused. He will not be able to clearly feel where you are directing him.

10. When you have changed direction left and right, stop, park and give your pony a rub.

When you can confidently and easily ask your pony to change direction to the left or to the right, you can start to introduce obstacles and challenges.

To the parent or guardian:

You can help young children by keeping them online and helping them to "see" and change direction.

Allow your pony to use his neck

When your pony makes a transition from trot to walk or walk to trot, he may lift his head and neck a little. This is because he uses his head and neck to help balance himself.

Until he is stronger and more balanced, it is OK to allow him to do this. As he becomes stronger and more balanced it is important that he uses his head and neck correctly so that he develops a strong back. **Then he can carry you!**

If you were to carry someone on your back when you were crawling on the floor, you would have to lift your back using your abdominal (tummy) muscles.

If you didn't, you would not be able to carry them comfortably. If your pony can not use his neck freely, he cannot use his tummy muscles correctly and this will affect how he uses his front and hind legs.

Important! If your pony continues to move with his head and neck in the air, then seek advice from a Think Like a Pony Instructor.

When your pony's head and neck are lower, he can use his tummy muscles.

If you are out of balance or your contact on the reins restricts your pony in any way, then he will not be able to use his head and neck. He may become tense and unwilling to go forward or unwilling to stop.

REMEMBER! The reins belong to your pony!

Make sure that you allow him to use his head and neck so that he can stretch his neck forward and round his back.

This does not mean that your reins have to be long.

You must allow him to move freely through the contact in your reins and by following his movement in your body. You will feel this movement through your backbone, rib cage and sternum.

11. Look ahead to your first obstacle and decide to trot to the left or right of it or through it.

12. As you approach the first obstacle, look for the next one. Set your intention and think about going there. Decide if the obstacle is going to be on your left or right or if you are going through it.

Looking for the next obstacle makes your pony aware of where you want to go next. If you look down at the obstacle, you may cause your pony to stop, become unbalanced or become concerned.

13. Keep looking up in the direction that will take you to your next obstacle. If your pony "wobbles" off his line and you are finding it difficult to keep him straight, check your intention and body language.

Are your nose, shoulders and belly button pointing in the same direction?

Are your legs in the correct place?

If they have slipped back, you will be talking to his hindquarters. This will confuse him.

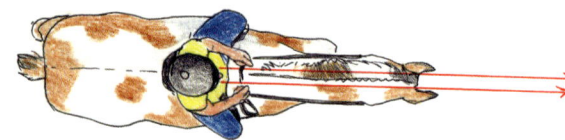

Ask your helper for feedback about your position.

REMEMBER! You are trying to direct and "steer" your pony's front end. Keep your legs on the girth, so you can use them to help direct and turn your pony. Your feet should be "reaching" for the floor and your weight balanced over the balls of your feet.

Always use your intention and body language before your reins.

The exercises in this chapter are explained and supported through worksheets and video lessons, which are available through the **Think Like a Pony Club.**

Keep it simple and make sure it is fun for both of you!

Chapter 8
Diagonals

When your pony is trotting, you should feel him spring from one diagonal pair of feet to the next.

"The left diagonal" describes the movement of the left front leg and the right hind leg as they rise and lift off the ground.

"The right diagonal" describes the movement of the right front leg and the left hind leg as they rise and lift off the ground.

It is important to understand your pony's diagonal movement to help you to rise and sit in balance and to help your pony to be strong and balanced.

When you are doing "rising trot", you are in time with one diagonal pair of legs. When they rise, you rise when they return to the ground, you sit.

Diagonals and rising trot

Rising and sitting on diagonals feels natural because as your pony prepares to step underneath with his hind leg, his barrel will swing and lift you out of the saddle.

Your pony may prefer you to sit when one diagonal pair touches the floor rather than the other. This shows you that he has one side that is stronger than the other. If you only ever sit on one diagonal, you will both become unbalanced because your pony will build stronger muscles on one side of his body. This will make your pony stiff and he will find it difficult to bend or turn.

To make sure you both stay balanced and use both sides of your body, it is important to change your diagonal regularly during your ride.

Circles

Sitting on the correct diagonal is especially important when you are riding a circle.

When you ride a circle to the left, you should be sitting when the right diagonal is touching the ground. To check that you are doing this, you can glance down at your pony's shoulders and check that you are sitting as his outside shoulder moves backwards.

When you are on the correct diagonal, you will be sitting as his inside hind leg is on the ground. You will leave the saddle as your pony's leg is leaving the ground. This means that you can help him to push himself forward.

This helps him to become athletic and strong.

Now that your trot is more balanced and effortless, you can start to become aware of which diagonal you are on. When you are aware of this you can learn to change your diagonal.

Exercise 6. Riding the correct diagonal to the right

With adult supervision and in a safe place where you both feel comfortable:

1. With your halter and rope attached and your pony's saddle on, prepare him to ride.

2. When you are ready, mount your pony and go through your checklist.

- Relax
- Flex
- Position
- Allow

3. When you are ready, ask your pony to walk on, then trot in rhythm so that you can feel his diagonal spring.

4. If you are in an arena or paddock, trot to the right.

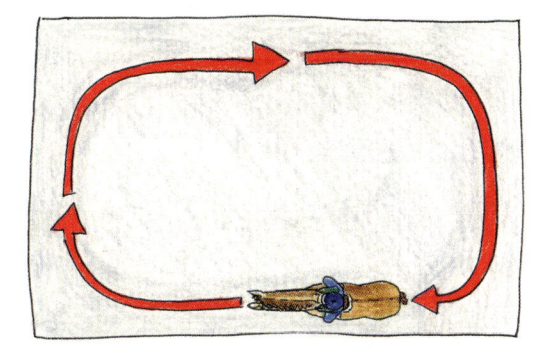

Your right hand will be on the inside of the arena.

Your left hand will be on the outside.

5. Now glance at your pony's shoulder. You should be sitting as his outside shoulder comes back. The outside shoulder is the one closest to the fence or hedge.

If you are sitting when his inside shoulder comes back, you are on the wrong diagonal. To correct this, you can sit for two beats.

Say out loud "sit, sit".

When you have sat for two beats, look down and check that you are sitting when the left shoulder comes back. This will mean that you are moving in time with the left diagonal.

You may already be sitting as his outside shoulder moves back. This means that you are on the correct diagonal.

When you sit for two beats (sit-sit), it does not matter if you bounce a little bit at this stage.

REMEMBER! If you are sitting as his left shoulder comes back, you are on the correct diagonal.

Do 2-4 laps on this diagonal then stop and park your pony.

Getting the right diagonal takes practise. You and your pony have done well.

Try not to stop near the gate or he may think he has finished and is going out.

Exercise 6a. Riding the correct diagonal to the left

1. When you are ready, ask your pony to walk on, then trot in rhythm so that you can feel his diagonal spring.

2. If you are in an arena or paddock, trot to the left.

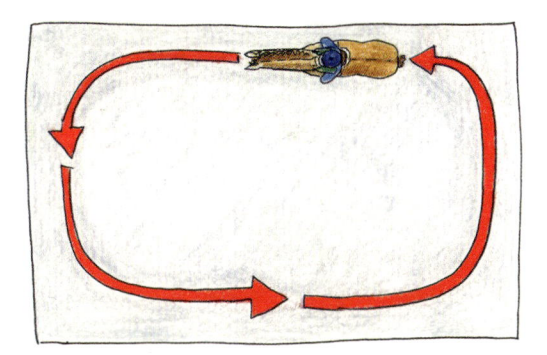

> Your left hand will be on the inside of the arena.
>
> Your right hand will be on the outside of the arena.

3. Now glance at your pony's shoulder. You should be sitting as his outside shoulder comes back. If you are sitting when his inside shoulder comes back, you are on the wrong diagonal. To correct this, you can sit for two beats.

Say out loud "sit, sit".

When you have sat for two beats, look down and check that you are sitting when the right shoulder comes back. This will mean that you are moving in time with the right diagonal.

You may already be sitting as his outside shoulder moves back. This means that you are on the correct diagonal.

In time, with practise, you will be able to feel which diagonal you are on and just glance down to check.

You will then learn to use this feel to rise on the correct diagonal.

Now that you can change from one diagonal to the other, you can ride simple patterns at trot. These will help your pony to become relaxed, supple and balanced.

Exercise 6b. Change the rein

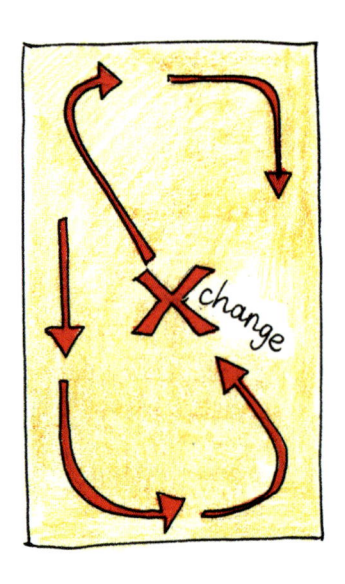

You are going to ask your pony to trot the pattern in the diagram.

You could mark the middle with a cone or safe obstacle.

1. Whatever the shape of the arena or paddock you are in, you are going to trot through the centre to change direction. As you approach the centre, you are going to change your diagonal. Sit for two beats you can say out loud "sit-sit".

As you approach the marker, change your diagonal before you change direction. This way you will be on the correct diagonal when you turn.

Use your body language and intention to prepare your pony to turn. If he does not respond to your body language, you can use your reins to guide and direct him.

You and your pony should move and turn together!

Make sure that you both stay on the track you intended to ride.

Exercise 6c. Serpentines and S patterns

Set out three markers like in the picture. This pattern is more complicated than the last so to prepare, walk the pattern first before you trot.

1. First walk the pattern starting on the left rein and then, when you are ready, ask your pony to trot. Trot one full circle and then prepare to start your serpentine.

2. At the first obstacle, change your intention and body language and ride across the arena.

3. When you reach the middle of the arena, change your diagonal by sitting for two beats. Say out loud "sit-sit".

REMEMBER! When you are on the left rein, you will sit as the right shoulder comes back.

4. Before you reach the arena fence, turn your **head, shoulders, knees and toes** to the right to direct your pony to the right.

   Ride around your second marker and then ride straight across the arena.

5. When you reach the middle of the arena, change your diagonal by sitting for two beats. Say out loud "sit-sit"

6. Before you reach the arena fence, turn your **head, shoulders, knees and toes** to the left to direct your pony to the left.

   You should now be back on the left rein. If you changed your diagonals correctly, you will still be sitting as the right shoulder comes back. You can glance down to check.

If you do not have a lot of space, you may only be able to do 2 loops. That's OK.

Check that your contact is shared and allowing your pony forwards. Make sure you are using your reins correctly, one rein at a time, then back to neutral.

The exercises in this chapter are explained and supported through worksheets and video lessons, which are available through the Think Like a Pony Club.

Have fun!
Make sure that you show your pony that you appreciate his efforts!

Chapter 9
Trot on a circle

Now you can trot in balance and rhythm with your pony, change diagonals and change direction, you are prepared to trot a circle.

It seems like a simple thing to trot a circle while you ride your pony, but you know that asking your pony to walk a true circle when you rode him was not easy.

REMEMBER! Asking your pony to ride on a circle helps him to:

- Be relaxed.
- Become supple.
- Develop a rhythm.
- Use both sides of his body equally.
- Become more balanced.

Now your pony has to trot a circle and carry you!

He will find it especially difficult if you are not using your body language and intention correctly.

Now you are moving faster, you have to be more aware of your intention, body language and balance.

The leg and rein aids that you need to ask your pony to stay on a circle at trot are the same as when you ride a circle at walk.

Now that you are trotting it is more important that you ride a circle with your body language.

REMEMBER!

- Focus ahead onto a circle – to see a circle, you must look ahead.
- Make sure that your head, shoulders, knees and toes are on a circle.
- Think about where your nose and belly button are pointing.
- To think "step-push".

Exercise 7. Riding a circle at trot clockwise.

With adult supervision and in a safe place where you both feel comfortable:

1. With your halter and rope attached and your pony's saddle on, prepare him to ride

2. When you are ready, mount your pony and go through your checklist.
    - Relax
    - Flex
    - Position
    - Allow

3. When you are ready, trot a large circle about 20 metres in diameter to the right (in a clockwise direction). Check your diagonal, remember you should be sitting as your pony's outside shoulder comes back. The shoulder that is on the outside of the circle.

Imagine your belly button shining down his mane.

Use your intention, body language, weight and then rein to keep him on the track of the circle.

Try to look through your pony's ears.

If you need to use your inside rein to direct your pony's nose onto a circle, make sure that you do not pull your pony around the circle. Keep your fingers around your reins, with your hands in front of you. Allow him forward and try to keep them a pair.

REMEMBER! To use your body language before your reins, your legs guide your pony before your hands.

4. Keep your legs on the girth and feel that you can guide his shoulders with your legs, weight and then the reins.

Make sure you look over the tips of his ears as you turn your shoulders on the circle.

You should be focusing on where you are going, moment to moment

The most important thing is that you and your pony keep your nose on the circle.

Make sure you breathe and smile!

Flex him when necessary, lift the inside rein to ask him to soften his jaw and look onto the circle.

Make sure that when you ask for flexion, your rein does not come into your body because this will give a backwards feel.

Check that you are only using enough lift in the rein to ask him to flex onto the circle.

The feel of your contact is like 'holding his hand' with the outside rein. Keep this feel steady, supporting him on the circle.

Hold the contact on the outside rein, making sure that you don't pull back. Think forward with your hands.

Feel you can release the inside rein when he has flexed, making sure that you do not drop or let go of the rein.

It does not matter how many times you need to ask him to flex and to look onto the circle. Make sure that you always put the rein back to neutral.

Think that your pony can draw a circle on the ground with his nose.

You should be able to look down at your pony and see both of his eyes. If you can only see one, he may be flexed too far. **This pony is flexed too far!**

You want his neck to follow his nose, his shoulders to follow his neck, his ribs to follow his shoulders and his hindquarters to follow his ribs.

REMEMBER! Your pony's nose should be in line with the middle of his chest. Just as if you were asking him to do a circle on the ground.

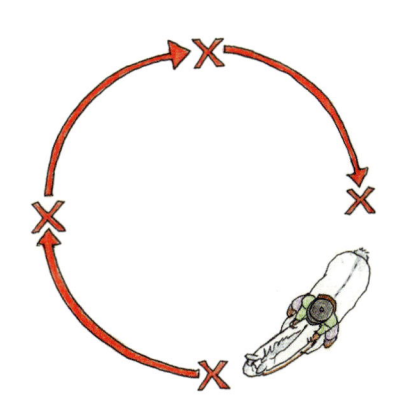

REMEMBER:

- Your legs on either side provide a tunnel for your pony to ride through.
- Your hips affect your legs.
- Your shoulders affect your hips.
- Your arms and hands help him to keep his head and neck in the middle of his shoulders.

5. When you can trot a circle, or you have improved the way you trot a circle, then ask your pony to walk.

Let him walk on a loose rein so he can stretch. This is a nice way to reward your pony for his efforts.

This pony is stretching.

If he keeps making the circle smaller, check that:

A) When you ask him to flex with the inside rein, that you are not asking him to flex too far.

If you take your rein too far out and away from his neck, you will unbalance him and cause him to step to the inside in order to rebalance himself.

B) You keep a steady contact on the outside rein to hold him on the circle. Check that this hold allows him forwards.

C) You are not trying to pull him around on a circle with your inside rein. If you feel that you need to pull him around the circle with the inside rein, then he is not listening to your body language and leg aids.

D) Make sure that you use your leg on the girth. If your leg slips behind the girth, your pony will think that you are talking to his hindquarters and will be confused. He may even try to take his hindquarters out of the circle which will push his shoulders onto the circle. **Think: step out onto the circle, if he does not respond, push him out onto the circle.**

If he keeps making the circle bigger, check that:

A) Your pony is flexing onto the circle. If you flex him too far or use your inside rein incorrectly, you may cause him to "run out of the circle" through his outside shoulder.

B) You are stepping your weight to the inside when necessary. You have to be focussed and determined to ride the circle so that your pony can follow your direction.

C) Your outside leg is on the girth with your toes pointing in the direction of the circle. Think that you can push the turn with your outside leg.

Practise riding a circle as often as you can. Ride 1 or 2 circles then rest. Circles are tiring for your pony if they are done correctly. Let him rest and build his strength and stamina. You do not need to be perfect, you just need to improve.

As you and your pony become more athletic, you can increase the number of circles from 2 to 4 then 4 to 6.

6. When you have ridden a few circles clockwise, ride a few circles anti-clockwise.

You may feel that your pony finds riding one way easier than the other. This is normal; just like you he will prefer to go one way. Keep practising so that he becomes strong and flexible on both reins.

If your pony finds trotting a circle difficult, ask your helper to work with you. Put a halter and line on with your bridle over the top. Ask them to help you to flex your pony and keep him on a circle.

You could even try...

A) Riding a figure of two fat circles, like a figure of eight.

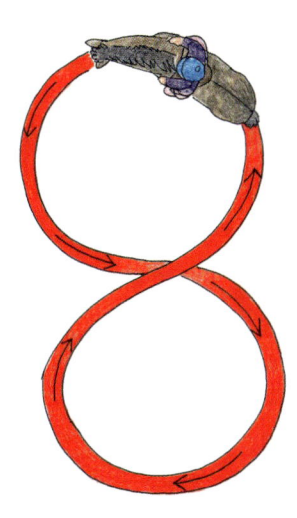

Change your diagonal at the centre obstacle. Use your intention, focus and body language to ride a figure of eight. All these exercises will improve your focus and your pony's suppleness, rhythm and balance.

If your pony is supple, balanced and has rhythm and you ride in balance, then together you will be able to make good transitions on a circle.

B) Asking your pony to trot half a circle and walk half a circle.

Allow him to move forward in his downward transition and check that you both stay on the circle. When he is doing well, reward him. Give him a rub or park him and have a rest together. It is not how many circles he does – it is how many good circles he does. Quality is better than quantity.

The exercises in this chapter are explained and supported through worksheets and video lessons, which are available through the **Think Like a Pony Club.**

Well done!

Chapter 10
Hindquarter Yield

When your pony can move his hindquarters around his forequarters, he is becoming more:

- Athletic
- Balanced
- Coordinated
- Flexible
- Strong

This is because he can move around his drive line without losing his balance.

When you can successfully ride this manoeuvre, you are also demonstrating that you are in control of your own body.

Riding this yield requires you to:

- Shift your weight.
- Position your body.
- Use steady pressure to ask your pony to move.
- Time your release to reward your pony for moving.
- Use your reins appropriately to help you to communicate with your pony if he finds this difficult.

This takes thought, planning, clear communication and maybe a little determination! These are all qualities of a good leader. Your pony may not find this easy so be prepared to take your time. Your pony will respect you more if you can achieve this manoeuvre so it is a win win for you both.

Exercise 8. Hindquarter yield from the ground

With adult supervision and in a safe place where you both feel comfortable:

1. With your halter and rope attached and your pony's saddle on, prepare him to ride

2. Before you ride this manoeuvre, first check that your pony can yield his hind quarters on the ground with his saddle on. Use steady pressure and reward each step that he takes.

By using steady pressure where your leg would be if you were riding, you are preparing your pony to understand pressure from your leg.

Position yourself by the drive line on the right hand side of your pony. Hold your reins as shown in the picture and place steady pressure behind the drive line where your leg could reach.

Only use your reins to control your pony if he moves forward. If he moves forward, lift your hand above his wither as you did with the rope halter in *Think Like a Pony on the Ground Workbook 2, Chapter 7*.

REMEMBER! Only ask your pony for one step at a time and give your pony a friendly rub after each step.

If your pony finds it hard to move his hindquarters, then use the right rein to ask him to flex a little.

Practise this yield on the ground from both sides.

REMEMBER! To Think Like a Pony! Ponies do not pull each other around, they push each other out of the way.

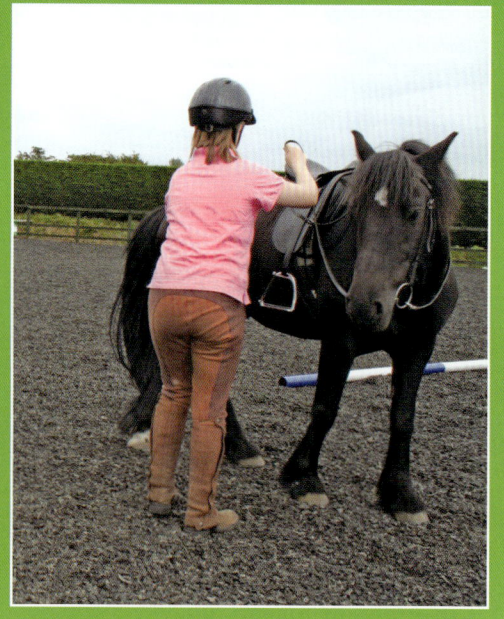

If your pony swishes his tail or shows any signs of pain or anxiety, check the fit of your saddle. You can ask your pony to yield his hindquarters without his saddle on to see if he finds this easier.

If he finds it easier, this is a sure indication that your pony's saddle feels uncomfortable.

Think Like a Pony in the Saddle Workbook 1 offers further advice as to how to assess the fit of your pony's saddle.

Exercise 8a. Hindquarter yield in the saddle

1. When you are ready, mount your pony and go through your check list:
- Relax
- Flex
- Position
- Allow

It is a good idea to walk forward and make a few turns and stops to give you time to tune into your pony and check that he is listening to you.

2. When you are ready, glance over your shoulder towards his left hind leg to bring your attention to his hindquarters.

As you do this, you will lighten your seat forward and your shoulders will turn so that your right shoulder moves forward and your left shoulder moves back.

This is your first signal.

This should only be a slight weight shift and turn, so be careful that you do not lean or tip too far. This would unbalance you and affect your weight aids.

3. Now place your left leg back towards your pony's hindquarters. Keep your knees in contact with your saddle.

Think push with your leg.

Use steady pressure from your leg to ask your pony to yield his hindquarters to the right. He may first step out with his right leg, then under with his left leg or he may first step under with his left leg and then out with his right leg.

It does not matter which order he steps his legs in, as long as he does step under his body with his left leg. This step under is what improves his strength, flexibility and coordination.

As soon as your pony makes a step to take his hindquarters away, release your pressure and put your leg back to the girth. Rub your pony and tell him he is a good boy.

Your right leg should stay at the girth to support your pony's shoulders and suggest that he does not try to step out or forward with his right front leg.

Your right rein should help to "hold" your pony still. It is important to make sure this is just a "hold" that stops your pony moving forward but there is no backward feel in the rein.

Think "contain" not "restrain."   **Think "hold" not "pull."**

If your pony does not yield and move his hindquarters when you apply pressure with your leg, you may need to:

A) Flex your pony with your left rein. This will make the manoeuvre easier for your pony.

B) If your pony still finds the manoeuvre difficult, lift your left rein out towards your pony's hindquarters.

Make sure that when you are using your rein, you continue to use your leg effectively.

Be careful not to pull him around with the rein or you will unbalance him.

Think **push** NOT pull.

C) Ask your helper to give you feedback on the manoeuvre and if necessary, they can tap towards your pony's hindquarters at the same time as you use your leg.

This motivates your pony to listen to your leg.

Make sure that your helper stops tapping when your pony does the right thing. Repeat the exercise until you do not need your helper to support your aids.

Make sure that once your pony has done the right thing, you release the pressure from your leg and look straight ahead. You can give your pony a friendly rub on his shoulder to let him know that you are pleased with his efforts.

If your pony takes one or two steps forward while he is learning to do the yield and carry you, that is OK.

If he continues to walk forward, he will not be able to step under with his hindquarters. To do an accurate hindquarter yield, your pony's forequarters must stay still.

If your pony finds this difficult then check:

- **Your position and body language- do not lean too far forward as this will unbalance your pony.**
- **You can hold your pony still with your right leg and right rein.**
- **You are putting pressure in the correct place with your left leg.**
- **You are releasing the pressure and rewarding your pony when he does the correct thing.**

When you can move your pony's hindquarters to the right, then ask him to move his hindquarters to the left.

Traditionally, a hindquarter yield is called a "turn on the forehand".

As your pony becomes more athletic, he will need less flexion, be able to keep his head and neck straight and he will find this yield easier. This takes teamwork!

Give yourself a pat on the back and your pony a rub as you have made a great achievement.

Asking your pony to yield and move his hindquarters can also be very useful when negotiating obstacles or passing through gates which you need to turn and close.

The exercises in this chapter are explained and supported through worksheets and video lessons, which are available through the Think Like a Pony Club.

Chapter 11
Forequarter Yield

When your pony can move his hindquarter around his forequarters, he is becoming more:

- Athletic
- Balanced
- Coordinated
- Flexible
- Strong

This is because he can move around his drive line without losing his balance.

For your pony to move their forequarters, he needs to shift his weight onto his hindquarters. This is because he can move around his drive line without losing his balance.

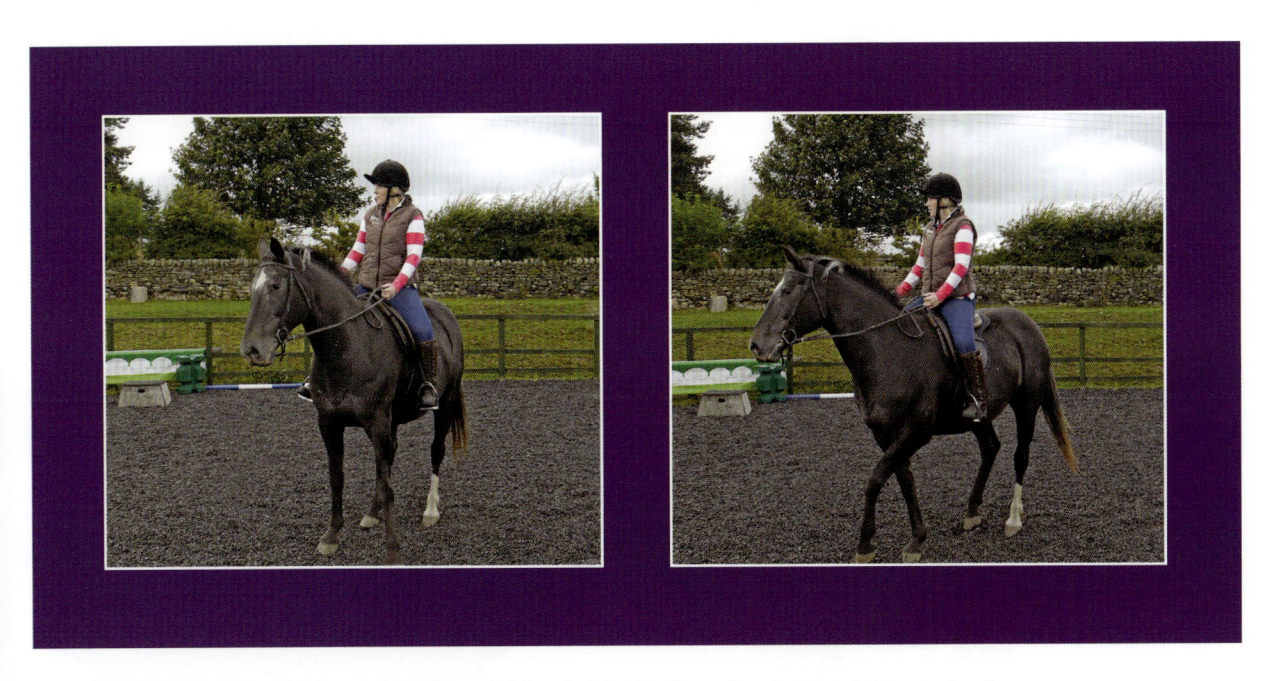

The best way to shift your pony's weight onto his hindquarters is to ask him to back up. This is because when a pony backs up, he will shift his weight off his forehand.

This pony has most of his weight on his forehand.

This pony has shifted his weight back to his hindquarters.

With his weight shifted onto his hindquarters, his forequarters are free to step out and across.

In **Think Like a Pony in the Saddle Workbook 1, Chapter 15,** you were asked to ride backwards and get in time with your pony's feet.

This is essential preparation for learning how to ask your pony to step his front legs out to the left or to the right.

REMEMBER! As you ride, you are sat at the drive line. This is like being sat in the driving seat. From here, you can influence your pony's movement but first you have to "think all the way down to his feet!"

Try this! Preparing for the forequarter yield

Try the following exercise to help you imagine that your feet are your pony's feet.

1. **Stand upright with your weight evenly balanced over each foot with your feet parallel and shoulder width apart. Keep your focus looking forward.**

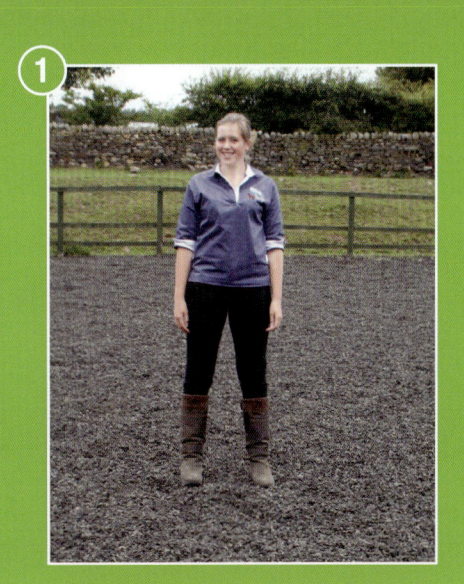

2. **Transfer your weight into your right foot. When you have felt this, step your left foot back.**

Do this slowly and purposefully so that you can remember the feeling.

After your left foot has stepped back, you should feel that your right foot is free to step where you direct it to.

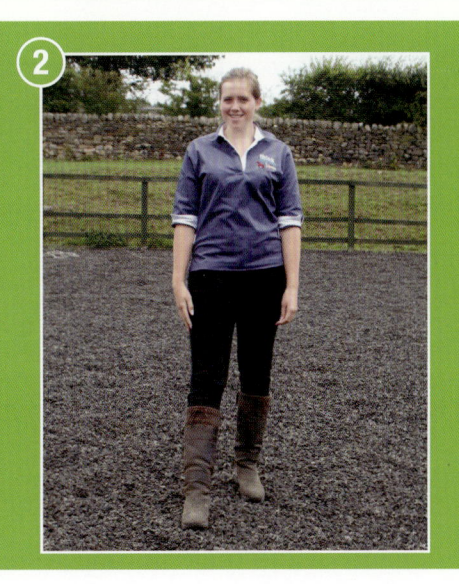

3. If you look forward, it is easier to influence your right leg to step back and behind you. As your right leg touches the floor, your weight transfers to this leg and your left leg is free.

Keep your shoulders straight so that you do not lean to one side as you will not feel the weight transfer.

This allows you to simulate how it feels to your pony as he takes diagonal steps back.

4. Go back to the beginning and stand upright with your weight evenly balanced over each foot, keeping your feet parallel and shoulder width apart.

Transfer your weight into your right foot so that you can step your left foot back.

After your left foot has stepped back, you should feel that your right foot is free to step where you direct it to.

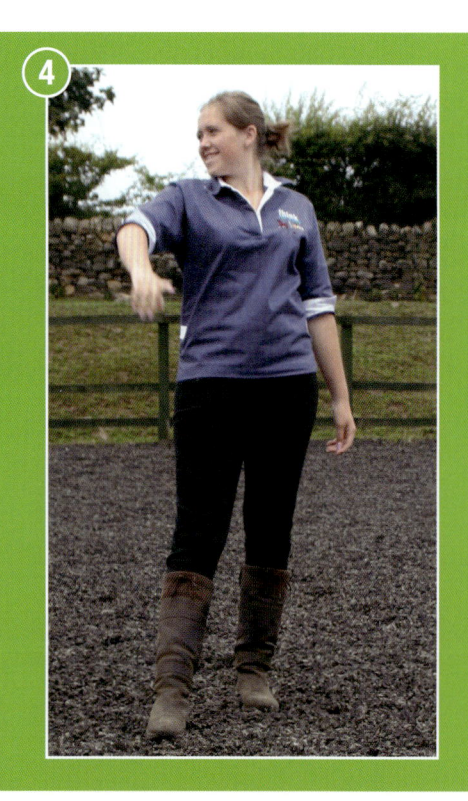

If you look up and point out to the right, you will easily influence your right leg to step to the right.

This allows you to simulate the feel of your pony turning his front end to the right after taking a backward step.

Looking in the direction that you are going helps you to change your weight and simulates your weight aid. Lifting your hand simulates your rein aid.

5. After you have looked up and stepped out to the right, transfer your weight onto your right leg.

This will free your left leg so that you can influence it to step to the right and cross over your right leg.

Lift your left hand and point in the direction which you are turning.

6. You are now going to think "step, turn, step, turn" as you rotate on the spot. It is important that you look up and into the direction which you are turning in as this affects your weight. Lifting and pointing your arms in turn simulates the feeling of your left rein then your right rein.

You should feel as if you are stepping into the new direction with your right leg and then pushing your left leg across your body. As your left foot touches the floor, you will feel a weight transfer which frees your right leg to step out again.

Keep looking in the direction in which you are turning.

This allows you to simulate what it feels like to turn your pony's forehand as he keeps his hindquarters still.

This is called a "turn on the haunches". You can repeat this sequence in both directions.

Experiment to see how it feels if you:

- **Look down**
- **Tilt your shoulders**
- **Lean forward**

This girl is looking down

Now she is tilting her shoulders

This will help you to understand the importance of having control of your body language. When you are clear with your body language, your pony can easily follow your direction.

REMEMBER! You and your pony are a mirror image of one another

When you have an understanding of how it will feel to ride this manoeuvre, you are prepared for the following exercise.

Exercise 9. Forequarter yield from the ground.

With adult supervision and in a safe place where you both feel comfortable:
1. **With your halter and rope attached and your pony's saddle on, prepare him to ride.**

2. Before you ride this manoeuvre, first check that your pony can yield his forequarters on the ground with his saddle on. Use steady pressure and reward each step that he takes. By using steady pressure where your leg would be if you were riding, you are preparing your pony to understand pressure from your leg.

Stand like the girl in the picture. Use your rein to ask your pony to back up but keep your focus up, making sure that you are looking in the direction that your pony is going to step.

Stepping your pony back asks him to shift weight onto his hindquarters so that he is able to step out with his right leg.

3. From this position, putting pressure on your pony's nose or head asks him to step out with his right leg.

Only use your reins to control your pony if he moves forward

Putting pressure on your pony's elbow or shoulder asks him to step across with his left leg.

If you need to remind yourself of how to do this yield from the ground, look at **Think Like a Pony on the Ground Workbook 2, Chapter 9.**

If your pony finds this difficult or shows any signs of discomfort, check:

- **Your position.**
- **You are asking your pony to step back before he steps out.**
- **You are in time with your pony's feet and not pushing him.**

If you are getting all of this check list correct and your pony still finds this manoeuvre difficult, check your saddle. If it is too tight around his shoulders or around the withers, this manoeuvre will be either painful or impossible!

To assess your saddle, you can ask your pony to yield his forequarters without his saddle on to see if he finds this easier. If he finds it easier, this is a sure indication that your pony's saddle feels uncomfortable and is restricting his movement.

It is very common for a pony's saddle to be too tight over the withers and around the shoulders. If your pony's saddle is too tight, it will also affect their turns and circles.

Think Like a Pony in the Saddle Workbook 1 offers further advice as to how to assess the fit of your pony's saddle.

When a saddle is tight or a pony's shoulders are sore, they will often refuse to bring their leg forward to cross in front of their body and will try to cross behind.

This can also happen if you are tense in the saddle or you have too much backward feel in your body and rein.

If your pony is crossing behind, you could rub him around the shoulders, withers and neck and go through your "carrot stretches" to help him. Refer to **Think Like a Pony in the Saddle Workbook 1, Chapter 1** for more guidance on "carrot stretches".

If you are unsure, seek professional advice from a **Think Like a Pony Instructor.**

Exercise 9a. Forequarter yield in the saddle

1. When you are ready mount your pony and go through your checklist:

- Relax
- Flex
- Position
- Allow

It is a good idea to walk forward and make a few turns and stops to give you time to tune into your pony and check that he is listening to you.

2. Ask your pony to come to a halt. Before you think about asking your pony to move his front end across, prepare yourself by simulating the body language you are going to use.

3. When you are ready, take a few steps back and think about getting in time with your pony's front feet. Feel when each front foot is about to lift off the floor.

When you are happy that you can feel this, you are going to prepare yourself to ask your pony to step his forequarters to the right. Take a moment to think about the manoeuvre as your pony backs up. Get in time with his feet and get ready to look to the right. Looking up to the right gives your pony the correct weight aid and lets him know that you want him to move his forequarters.

You can imagine that you are sitting on his hindquarters and asking them to stay still. Opening your chest and sitting tall will also help with this manoeuvre.

Be ready to lift your rein to direct your pony's front right foot.

4. When you feel that you are in time with your pony's feet, prepare to step out.

Imagine that you and your pony can step your right foot out together.

Keep the thought in your head.
Step out in time together.

Be careful not to lean with your shoulders or you will give the wrong weight aid. Just keep looking up into the direction you would like to go.

Use your rein to help you to **suggest** your pony lifts his right leg up and out.

Stay relaxed and focused and just feel that you and your pony can move together. If you stiffen or try too hard, your pony will resist you.

5. When you have felt your pony step out, prepare to ask him to step his left leg across his body.

Use your left leg to feel you can push your pony's left leg across and **infront** of his body. You can suggest with your left rein that he lifts his leg over and across.

6. You need to push your pony's left leg forward and across his body; this should not take a lot of effort, just good timing and a feel that suggests "this way please!"

Keep the thought in your head- "Step across in time together..."

Think step...push...

The rider is pushing her pony's leg across his body.

It is important that you keep your left leg at the girth and use it to push your pony across. If your leg moves back, it will be "talking" to his hindquarters. You may need to lift your left rein against your pony's neck to help him to lift his left leg off the floor.

Take care not to cross the rein across his withers or pull back.

Ask your helper to give you feedback on the manoeuvre. If necessary, they can tap towards your pony's forequarters at the same time as you use your leg. They can also help to stop your pony from moving forward.

This motivates your pony to listen to your leg.

Make sure that your helper stops tapping when your pony does the right thing. Repeat the exercise until you do not need your helper to support your aids.

You can use your left rein with a feeling of "hold" if your pony tries to walk forward. If he walks forward, he will be moving his hindquarters and forequarters. This does not help to make him more athletic.

Remember this feeling of hold is like holding his hand.

Take your time as rushing may cause you to pull your pony across when you ask for the yield. This will confuse him as you will not be in time with his feet and he will lose confidence and balance.

This girl is trying to pull her pony and because of this the pony is trying to move forwards.

The better your pony backs up, the more he will be willing and able to take his weight back and step out and across. If you are finding this manoeuvre difficult, improve your back up so you can better influence your pony's turn.

Check that your position, focus and use of rein are accurate. The better your position and focus, the easier your pony will find this turn.

When you feel your pony take a step to the right and place his foot out and down, you will have started to change direction.

When your pony takes this step, give him a rub.

It is not always easy to complete this manoeuvre so achieving this together is fantastic.

Practise this a few times and try to get your timing as accurate as possible. If your pony finds this difficult, check that:

- You can easily back up together. The better you back up, the easier you and your pony will find this yield.
- You are looking up in the direction in which you want your pony to step.
- You are lifting your right rein in time with his right foot.
- You are not leaning your shoulders.
- You are in time with your pony's feet.

7. When you can confidently step to the right, think about stepping left. Take a moment to prepare yourself and then step back and to the left with your pony's left leg leading.

When your pony steps out and across, you have changed direction. You can then walk forward.

A forequarter yield is a very athletic move so make sure that you only ask your pony for 1 leg step out, 1 leg step across and then rest.

Eventually, your pony will be able to do a full forequarter yield to the left and to the right. Traditionally, a forequarter yield is called a "turn on the hindquarters". This takes teamwork!

Give yourself a pat on the back and your pony a rub as you have made a great achievement. Asking your pony to yield and move his forequarters can also be very useful when negotiating obstacles or passing through gates which you will need to turn and close.

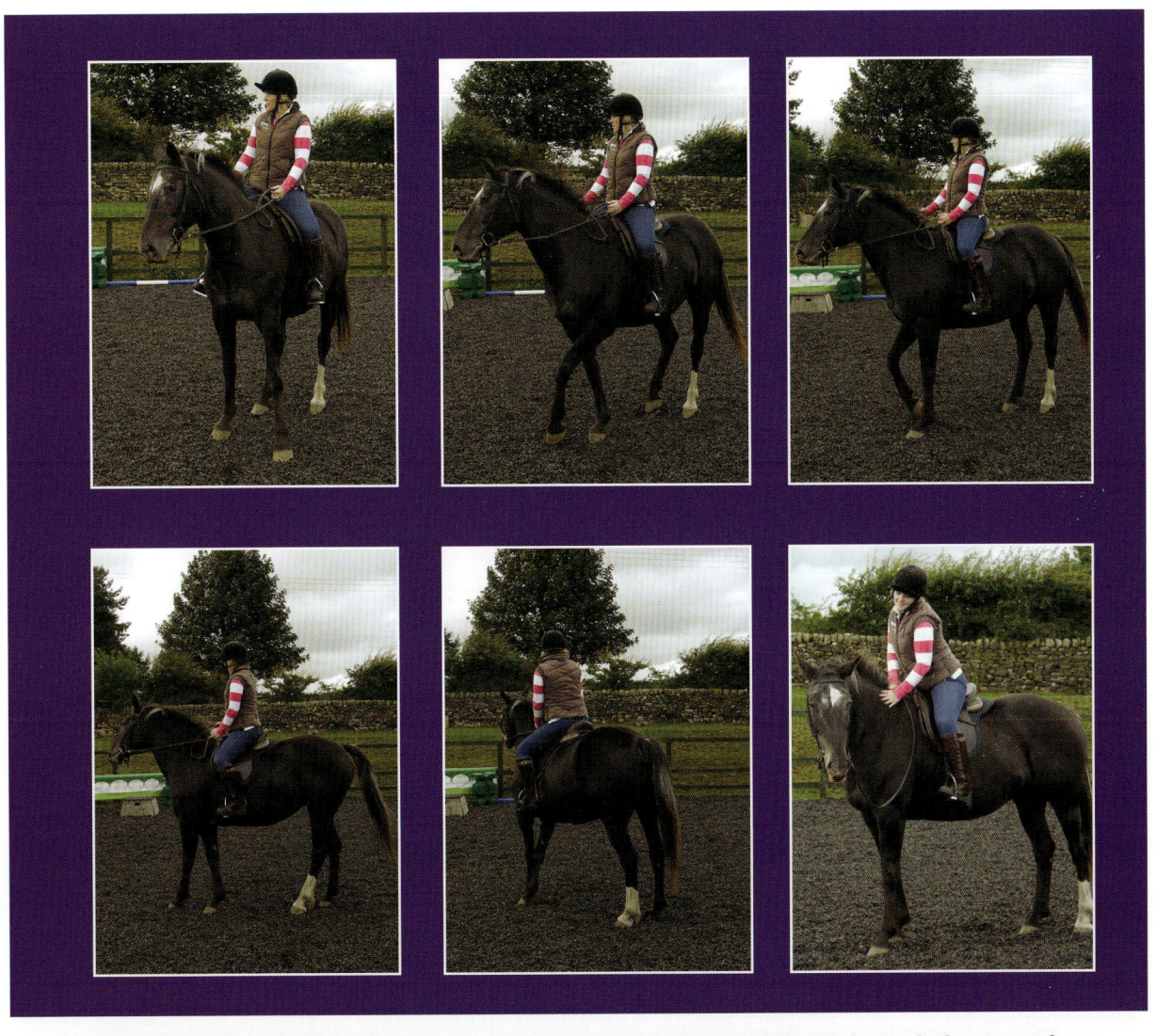

The exercises in this chapter are explained and supported through worksheets and video lessons, which are available through the Think Like a Pony Club.

Well done!

Chapter 12
Moving Sideways

When a pony steps sideways, they move their front end (forequarters) and back end (hindquarters) together.

To move sideways like this, your pony must be supple and able to coordinate his legs.

Taking steps sideways on the ground before you ride builds strength and helps your pony to become athletic. It also prepares your pony to move sideways away from your leg when you are riding.

This is called a "leg yield" because you are using your leg to push your pony onto a new path.

When you ask your pony to step in and out on a circle, you are leg yielding and moving sideways and forwards at the same time. In Think Like a Pony on the Ground Workbook 3, Chapter 4 you have already practised asking your pony to step in and out of a circle.

If you have found riding circles difficult, then asking your pony to move sideways will help you both to improve.

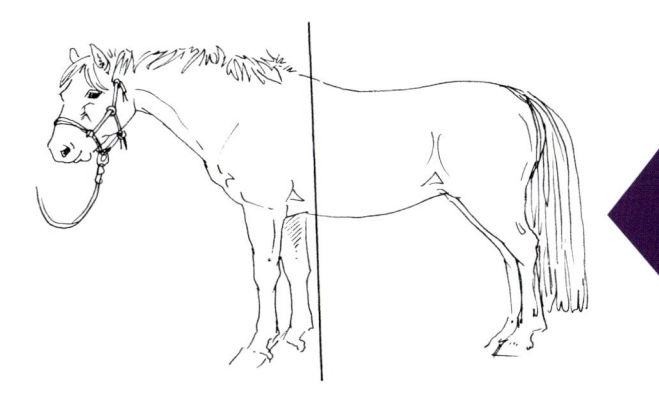

> When you ask your pony to move sideways, you need to put pressure on the drive-line because you want to push the forequarters and hindquarters together. When you ride, you will use steady pressure from your leg on the drive line to ask your pony to move sideways.

It is easier and safer to work on the ground using a signal.

This is because:

1. Ponies use signals before steady pressure.
2. Your pony is outside your personal space.

On the ground, your focus should be through the drive line and in this position it is easy to see what your pony's head, forequarters and hindquarters are doing.

Important safety issue: Essential preparation for this exercise is understanding how to yield the forequarters and hindquarters and being able to ask your pony to move out on a circle. This information is in Think Like a Pony on the Ground Workbooks 2 and 3.

When you ask your pony to move sideways he will want to walk forwards.
This may be because he is:

- **Confused and he may think that you want him to walk forwards.**
- **Trying to be a leader and controlling direction.**
- **Uncomfortable and he may find sideways difficult so takes the easy option and walks forwards.**

Using a fence, wall or hedge to act as a barrier can help your pony to understand that you do not want him to go forwards.

It is very important that the barrier you are using is safe and high enough so your pony can not jump it or push it over.

Sideways can be difficult so you must:

1. Go slowly
2. Use phases
3. Reward your pony for trying

If you rush or forget to use phases, your pony may panic and this may cause him to
Before you start asking your pony to move sideways:

1. Check his hindquarters and forequarter yields using a signal.
2. Check he is comfortable facing your chosen barrier.

Your pony needs to be able to see the direction he is travelling.

Because of the position of his eyes on his head, he need only to be looking either straight ahead or slightly flexed in the direction that he is going.

In order to be balanced as he steps sideways, your pony needs to step out into the direction of travel with his leading leg as he did when he yielded his forequarters.

Try this! Preparing to go sideways

1. **Stand upright with your weight evenly balanced over each foot with your feet parallel and shoulder width apart. Keep your focus looking forward.**

2. **Now, try to step sideways to the right while looking to the left.**

   When you step and look in the opposite direction you will feel unbalanced and uncoordinated. This simulates what it may feel like if your pony tried to step to the right while looking to the left.

3. **Now, look up to the right and step to the right, leading with your left leg taking the first step across your right leg.**

   You will feel out of balance and may feel as if you are falling to the right. This simulates what it may feel like for your pony to step out of balance.

4. Now, look up to the right and you will feel your weight shift into your left leg. When you have felt this, step sideways leading with your right leg.

When your right leg has touched the floor, step your left leg across your body.

This simulates the weight shift that your pony will make to step in balance and move sideways. This will feel natural and coordinated.

Your pony may be able to look in the wrong direction and move sideways or step out of balance but he wouldn't be able to move correctly. He may develop a twist in his body, become unbalanced or uncomfortable

Helping your pony to find this manoeuvre comfortable and effortless from the ground will help him to become confident and willing when you try the manoeuvre in the saddle.

> If you rush your pony and do not give him time to think, he will become confused mentally, emotionally and physically!

Exercise 10. Moving sideways on the ground

With adult supervision and in a safe place where you both feel comfortable:

1. With your halter and rope attached and your pony's saddle on, prepare him to ride.

2. Before you ride this manoeuvre, first check that your pony can move sideways from a signal on the ground with his saddle on.

Even if you followed the Think Like a Pony on the Ground series, you will have never asked your pony to move sideways before so it is important that you follow these instructions carefully.

3. Stand at your pony's shoulder and lead him towards the barrier, like the girl in the picture.

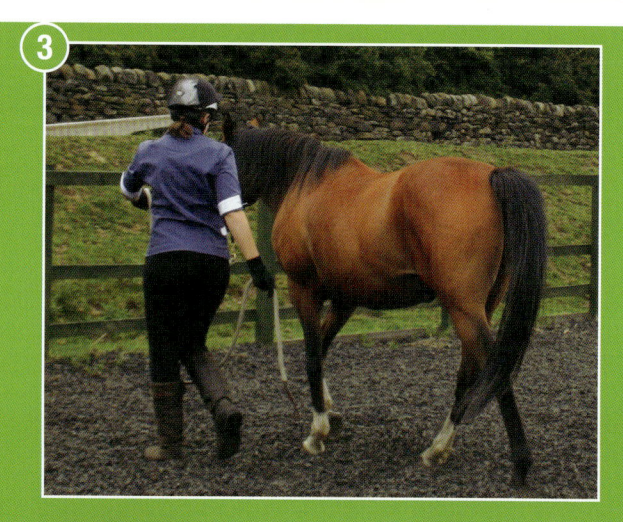

As you approach the barrier, turn to face your pony's shoulder. Make sure that your pony is outside your personal space.

4. Direct your focus up and over the drive line and use your left hand to signal him to look away from you.

5. As he looks away use the tail of your rope in your right hand to signal to him to move away from you. Use a slow and steady action towards the drive line. Give him time to try to respond. It is important that your signal and focus are through the drive line.

Be patient. Rushing may cause your pony to panic. He has nowhere to go because there is a barrier preventing forward movement. Give him time to work out what you want.

If your pony feels or looks as if he is about to walk away from you up the fence then. "Check" him with a feel on the line Make sure that you are not pulling him towards you.

This pony has made one sideways step.

As he becomes coordinated, he will move his forequarters and hindquarters together, stepping under his body with his left hind leg and out with his right front leg.
Finally out with his right hind leg and across with his left front leg.

Be determined, stay focused and slowly go through your phases. Touch your pony with the rope with a swinging rhythm if he does not attempt to step sideways. Make sure that you do not step towards your pony.

If he looks back at you, it is very important to ask him to look where you are asking him to step. Use your left hand to signal to him to look away from you.

This is an important safety issue.

If you feel your pony feels as if he is going to run away down the fence or barrier, you have to ask him to slow his front end down. Sometimes just a close of the hand or a lift in the line is enough.

If your pony turns away from you so that his bottom is facing you, then you cannot "push" on the drive line.

Take hold of the rope and walk backwards. Ask your pony to stop and start again.

If he looks at all anxious or confused, you can reassure him by isolating the problem.

Ask him to move his front end (forequarters)
Ask him to move his back end (hindquarters)

Then try going sideways again.

6. Make sure that you practice this exercise moving in both directions. Your pony may not be able to move to the left and to the right equally but if you practise, this will improve.

If your pony found moving sideways difficult, it is OK to allow him to move at an angle as long as he does not straighten his body too much and try to pull away down the barrier or bring his hindquarters too close to you. This also prevents some pony's worrying about the barrier.

As long as you continue to put pressure on the drive line and control where he is looking, he will straighten up.

Do not try to put pressure in front of or behind the drive line to straighten your pony!

The moment your pony tries to step away from you, stop signalling and rub him. This shows he is really listening to you and is trying to make sense of your signals.

Repeat this a few times making sure you only ask for 1 or 2 steps at a time. This will give your pony time to coordinate himself. If you rush he may bang into himself in an effort to move away from you.

This is a big achievement! *Well done!*

8. Before you ride this exercise, check that your pony can move sideways in his saddle

You are now ready to ride a sideways step!

Exercise 10a. Moving sideways in the saddle

1. When you are ready, mount your pony and go through your checklist.

- Relax
- Flex
- Position
- Allow

2. Ask your pony to walk on, then do a few hindquarter and forequarter yields. When you are ready walk towards the barrier.

As you reach the barrier turn to look to the right and think about moving sideways to the right. Looking up to the right will shift your weight.

Keep your shoulders level. Leaning will put your weight in the wrong place.

3. Think about you and your pony stepping to the right. Make sure you are looking to the right.

To help him to understand this, be ready to step in time with him and use your reins in time with your legs.

Feel you can step out with your right leg and guide your pony with your right rein.

4. Push with your left leg on the girth and guide your pony with your left rein. Be careful not to take your left rein across your pony's withers.

Keep your leg on the girth, stepping and pushing in time with your pony's movement.

If your pony steps his front end and leaves his hindquarters behind, then you can put your left leg back and push his hindquarters across to help him to straighten up.

Make sure that your focus always remains up and looking to the right.

Ask you helper to give you feedback on the manoeuvre. If necessary, they can help by giving a rhythmical signal towards your pony's drive line. This motivates your pony to listen to your leg.

Make sure that your helper stops signalling when your pony does the right thing. Repeat the exercise until you do not need your helper to support your aids.

Moving sideways together takes timing and feel. You have to feel where your pony's feet are and feel what his next step is so that you can time when to ask and when to reward. If you are finding sideways difficult go back to stepping sideways on a circle. When you can feel this try again from halt.

Ponies often swish their tail or lift their head because this is one of the most difficult manoeuvres that you are asking them to do, so be patient.

Moving sideways is fun but requires strength and coordination so try a little at a time.

When your pony understands and is able to go sideways, he will not lift his head or swish his tail.

Be careful not to pull your pony; this will cause him to become unbalanced and he may try to walk backwards. He may even bang into himself.

When you feel a sideways step, stop and reward your pony. Give him a rub and a moment to stop and think.

Well done!

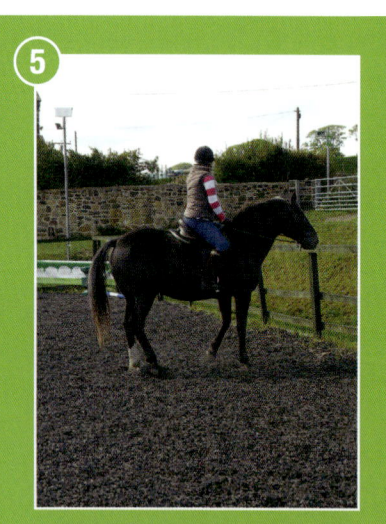

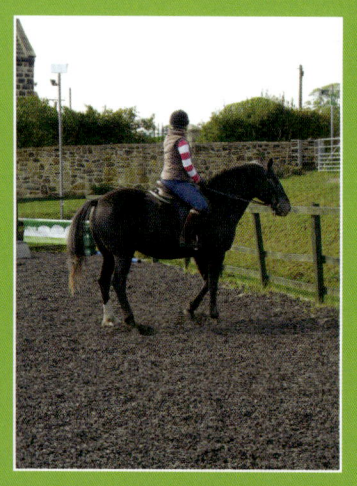

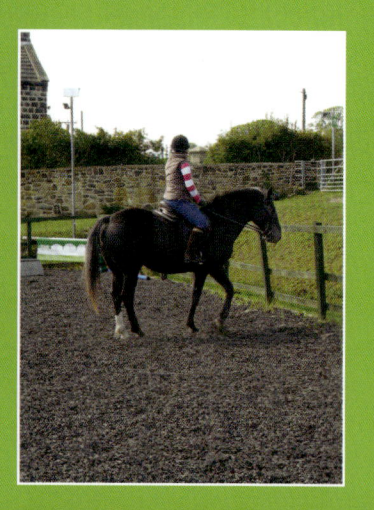

5. When you can step to the right then repeat the exercise to the left.

Eventually you will be able to move sideways without a barrier. If your pony walks forward, hold him first with your body, then your rein. Stay focused and have fun.

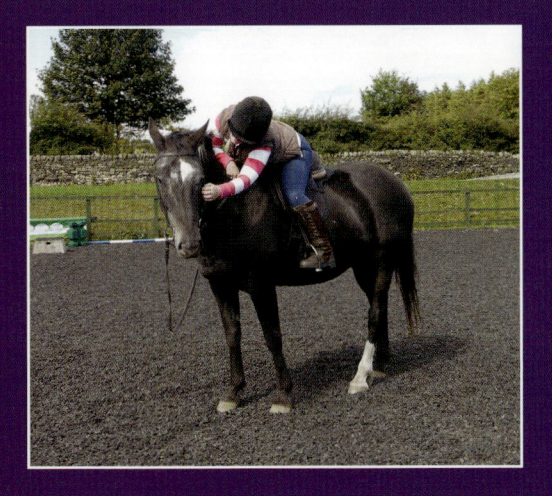

Eventually you will be able to move sideways without a barrier. If your pony walks forward, hold him first with your body, then one rein at a time.

Stay focused and have fun!

With this preparation, you can more easily learn to canter, prepare to hack out, jump and have fun together.

Nothing you do has to be perfect, just aim to get better each time you ride. That way you and your pony will keep having fun together!

The more you practise and prepare, the easier you will find the next step on your journey to becoming a good leader, friend and partner for your pony.

REMEMBER! All the information in the Think Like a Pony Workbooks is supported by worksheets and video lessons, which are available through the Think Like a Pony Club!

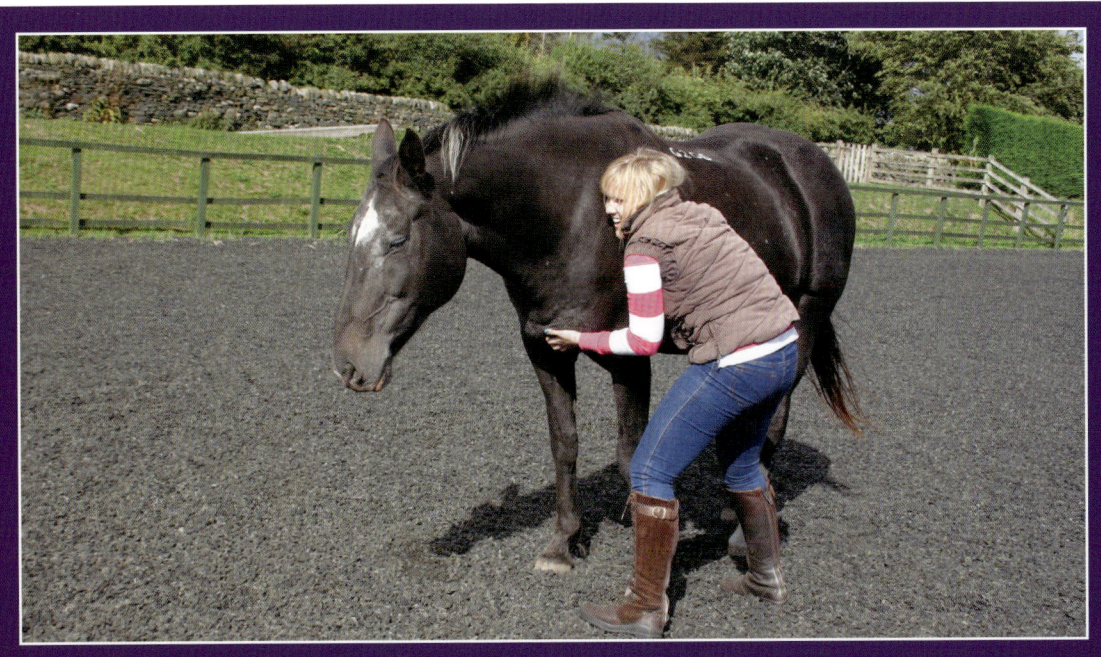

Wow - you have learned a lot.

You now have a better understanding of contact.

You are now becoming a responsible rider because you know that contact begins in the saddle.

You now accept that you communicate first with your body language, then with your reins. This way, your pony can make sense of the contact from your hand because it matches the signal from your body.

Contact shared by friends feels good!

Now that you understand contact, your pony is trusting you because they can make sense of what you are asking.

You are now a good leader, not only on the ground but in the saddle too.

You have worked hard to become more coordinated, balanced and straight.

You can now follow your pony's rhythm and movement.

Your riding feels effortless, fun and above all, safe!

The bond between you and your pony is growing because you understand what is needed to build a partnership.

You have gained your pony's respect so that applying the scales of training is natural and fun!

Love Lynn